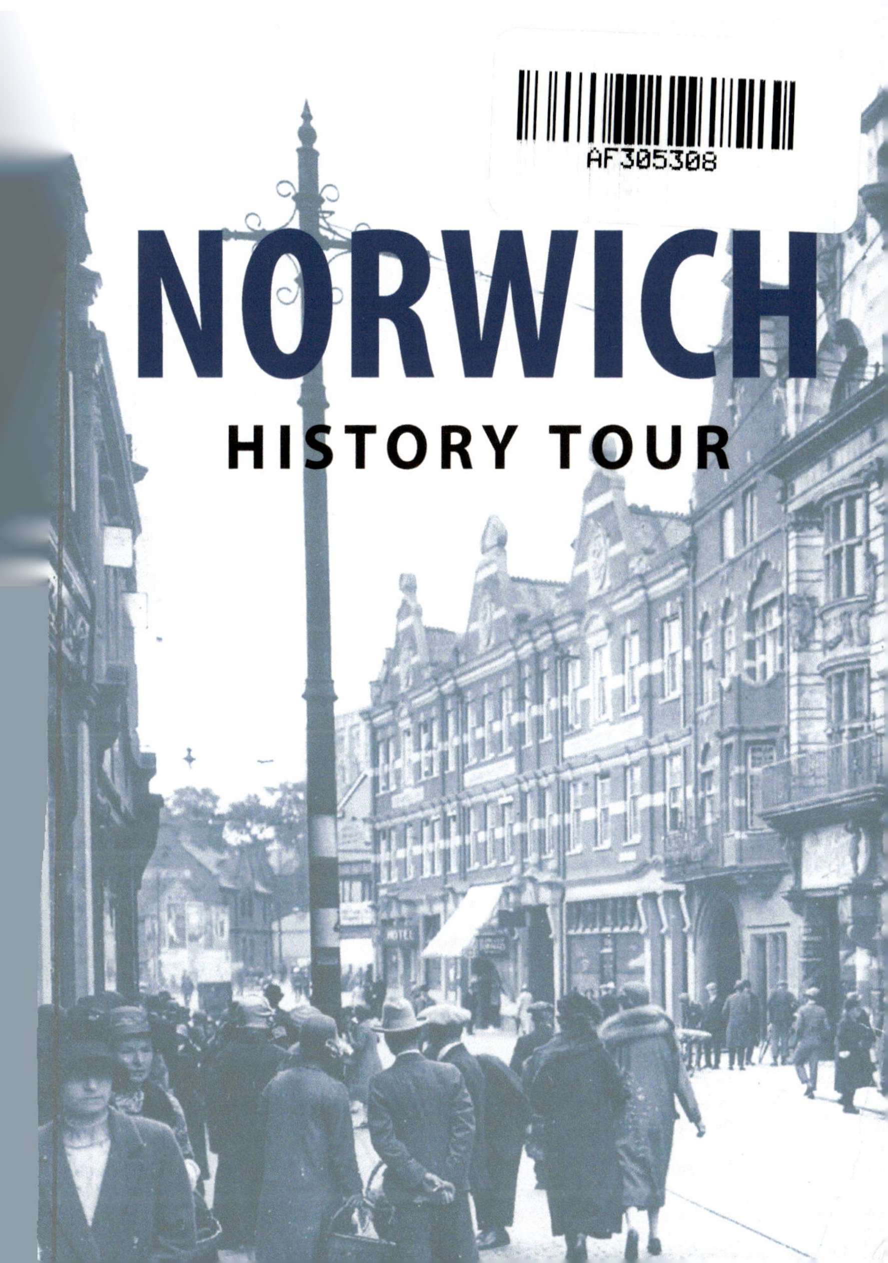
AF305308
NORWICH
HISTORY TOUR

First published 2010
This edition published 2014

Amberley Publishing
The Hill, Stroud,
Gloucestershire, GL5 4EP
www.amberley-books.com

ISBN 978 1 4456 4147 8 (print)
ISBN 978 1 4456 4161 4 (ebook)

British Library Cataloguing in
Publication Data.
A catalogue record for this book is
available from the British Library.

Typesetting by Amberley Publishing.
Printed in Great Britain.

Map on pages 6 & 7 courtesy of
OS Streetview.

Appointed GPSR EU Representative:
Easy Access System Europe Oü,
16879218
Address: Mustamäe tee 50, 10621,
Tallinn, Estonia
Contact Details: gpsr.requests@
easproject.com, +358 40 500 3575

INTRODUCTION

One of the first written mentions of Norwich is in the year 1004 when, according to the *Anglo-Saxon Chronicle*, the Viking king Sweyn sailed with his fleet up the river Wensum and burned Norwich to the ground. This introduces three themes that relate to the whole history of the city: the influence of Europe, the importance of the river and the vulnerability of the city to fire, flood, and enemy attack. The Vikings have left their mark on the city mainly in the form of street names: the 'gate' element in familiar streets like Colegate and Gildengate does not refer to any gate but is the Scandinavian word *gata*, meaning way or road.

The next group of settlers, however, completely altered the shape of the city and created the landscape that we see today. The Normans took over Norwich after 1066 and erected the two most iconic buildings in the city: the castle and the cathedral. Saxon houses and churches were pulled down to make way for them and the Saxon market, which had been in Tombland, was moved to the site in front of Saint Peter Mancroft where it still functions today, over nine centuries later.

For many centuries, Norwich was the largest town in England outside London. It had more churches than any other town and the longest medieval city wall. Its wealth was built on trade both throughout Norfolk and from Europe along the river, and Dragon Hall is a reminder of this activity.

Later, Norwich grew less fast and was overtaken by many of the industrial cities of the north. As well as its Anglican churches, it has a strong Nonconformist element, and the Society of Friends (Quakers) have also had a large community in the town. It has also had a proud reputation for welcoming in 'strangers', as they are known, and people from other countries; several thousand French- and Dutch-speaking immigrants came to Norwich in the 1560s and 1570s, bringing their own characteristics into the cultural mix, such as the tulip, the Dutch gable, and the canary, which became so beloved of Norwich folk over the centuries that the football club takes its popular name, the Canaries, from them. With these elements has come a reputation for charity and also for radicalism. Norwich was the first outside London to have a specialist hospital for those with mental health problems (the Bethel Hospital), and one of the first to set up an institution caring for the blind (now the Norfolk and Norwich Association for the Blind). 'Over the Water', the area north of the river, has developed its own personality over the centuries, and was the birthplace of two of the many women of character that the city has produced: Elizabeth Fry, the prison reformer, and Harriet Martineau, the writer.

The city's main wealth throughout history has come from weaving but an increasing diversity of businesses developed in the eighteenth and nineteenth centuries, some of which became known throughout Britain and the world. These have included

Norwich Union insurance (now Aviva), Colman's mustard, Caley's 'marching chocolate', Barclay's bank and Jarrold's the printers. The iron and steel making firms of Barnards' and of Boulton and Paul also established a worldwide fame, making products as diverse as barbed wire, aeroplanes, and cast-iron prefabricated churches!

Two twentieth century events that changed the shape of Norwich are covered in this book. The great flood of 1912 made people aware of the dreadful conditions in which many Norwich people lived, crowded around yards behind the main streets of the city. This led directly to the building of new housing estates after the First World War, like those at Mile Cross, Earlham and Lakenham; Norwich built more council houses than any city of its size. The Second World War saw considerable damage from bombing raids, especially the so-called Baedeker raids of April 1942. The changes this has produced in the city include the total rebuilding of Saint Stephen's shopping street. More recent decades have seen the development of two major new shopping centres, Castle Mall on and underneath the site of the former Cattle Market, which closed in the 1960s, and Chapel Field on the site of Caley's factory. As the factories along the river have closed in recent decades, they have been replaced by apartments and an ever-expanding river walk, one of the city's hidden delights.

Today's Norwich is a city where a medieval church can stand next to a twenty-first century shopping centre, and where a beer festival can take place in a medieval friary. This juxtaposition of past and present makes it a fascinating place for visitors and residents alike.

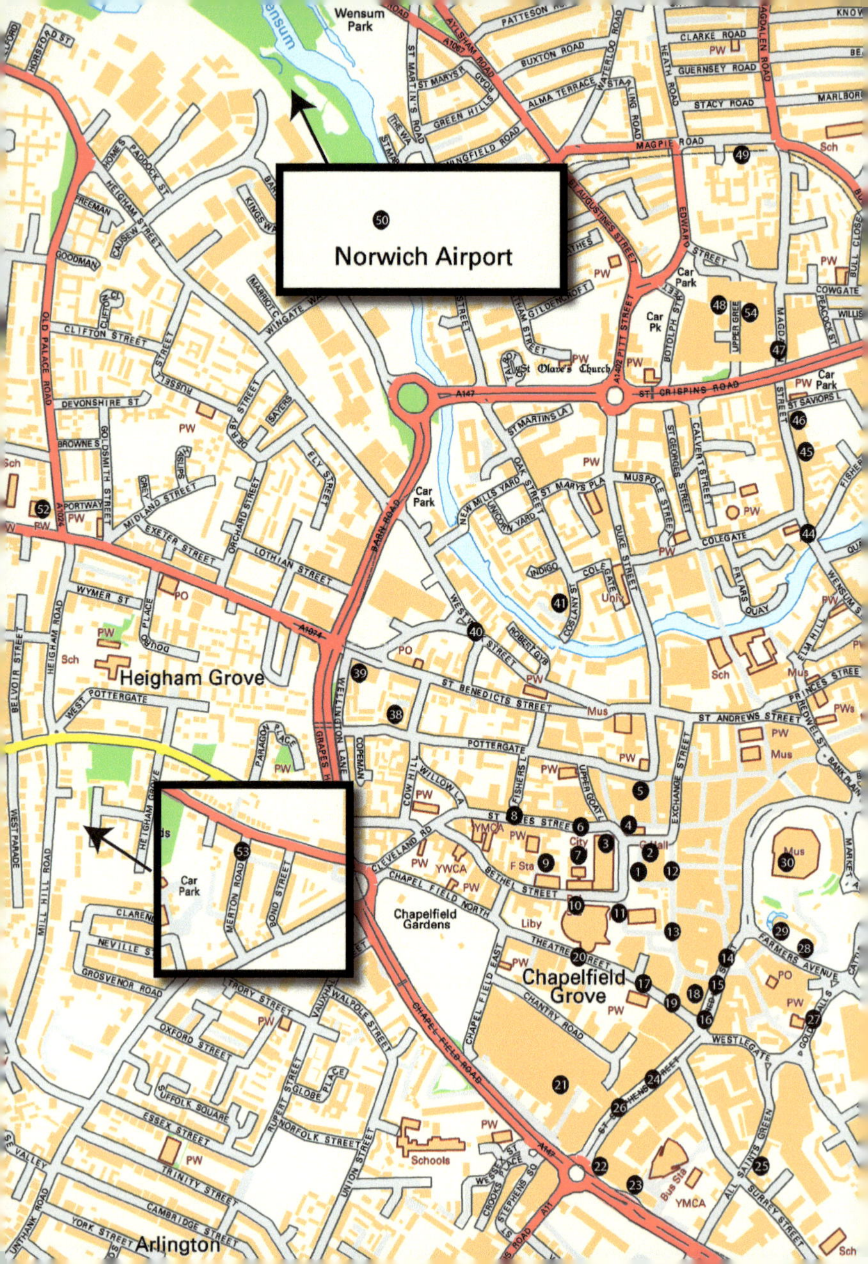
Wensum Park
Wensum
Norwich Airport
50
Heigham Grove
Arlington
Chapelfield
Grove
Chapelfield
Gardens
Chapelfield North
Chapel Field East
Old Palace Road
Clifton Street
Devonshire St
Browne's
Goldsmith Street
Portway
Midland Street
Exeter Street
Lothian Street
Orchard Street
Derby Street
Ely Street
Sayers
Wingate Way
Marjot C
Kings Way
Paddock St
Heigham Street
Causew Street
Russell Street
Grey Barn Road
Freeman
Goodman
Horsford St
Horford St
Clifford St
Wymer St
Douro Place
PO
PW
Sch
52
PW
Belvoir Street
Heigham Road
West Pottergate
West Parade
Mill Hill Road
Heigham Grove
Merton Road
Bond Street
Car Park
53
Clarence
Neville S
Grosvenor Road
Trory Street
Walpole Street
Vauxhall
Rupert Street
Globe Place
Oxford Street
Suffolk Square
Essex Street
Norfolk Street
Union Street
Valley Road
Urthank Road
York Street
Trinity Street
Cambridge Street
Wellington Lane
Grapes H
Copeman
Paragon Place
Cleveland Rd
Bethel Street
Chantry Road
Chapel Field Road
Theatre Street
Willow La
Coburg St
Fishers La
St Giles Street
YMCA
YWCA
F Sta
City
G Hall
Liby
Schools
Bus Sta
YMCA
St Stephens Rd
Stephens Sq
Crooks Place
Wessex Place
All Saints Green
Surrey Street
Westlegate
Farmers Avenue
Market
Goal Hill
Exchange Street
Upper Goat L
St Andrews Street
Pottergate
St Benedicts Street
Princes Stree
Redwell St
Bank Plain
Colegate
Friars Quay
Wensum S
Fishergate
St Saviors L
Car Park
Muspole Street
Calvert Street
St Georges St
Duke Street
Colegate
Coslany St
Indigo
Univ
New Mills Yard
Unicorn Yard
St Marys Pla
Oak Street
West Street
Robert Gyb
St Martins La
Car Park
St Olave's Church
St Crispins Road
A147
Botolph Street
Gildencroft
Pitt Street
A1402
Car Pk
Car Park
Talbot
Magpie Road
St Augustines Street
Edward Street
Magdalen Street
Cowgate
Peacock St
Bull Close
Upper Green
St Crispins Road
Car Park
St Saviors L
Mus
Sch
Sch
Mus
Mus
Mus
48
54
47
46
45
44
49
St Martin's Road
St Marys Road
Green Hills
Alma Terrace
Aylsham Road
A1067
Patteson Rd
Buxton Road
Waterloo St
Heath Road
Clarke Road
Guernsey Road
Stacy Road
Marlbo
Know
Be
Sch
PW
PW
PW
Longfield Road
Sch
Wingate Wa
Barn Road
A1024
A1074
PW
PW
PW
PW
PW
PW
PW
PW
PW
PW
PW
PW
PW
PW
PW
PW
PW
PW
PW
PO
PO
PO
Mus
30
5
8
6
4
3
2
1
12
9
7
10
11
13
14
15
16
17
18
19
20
21
22
23
24
25
26
27
28
29
39
38
40
41
42

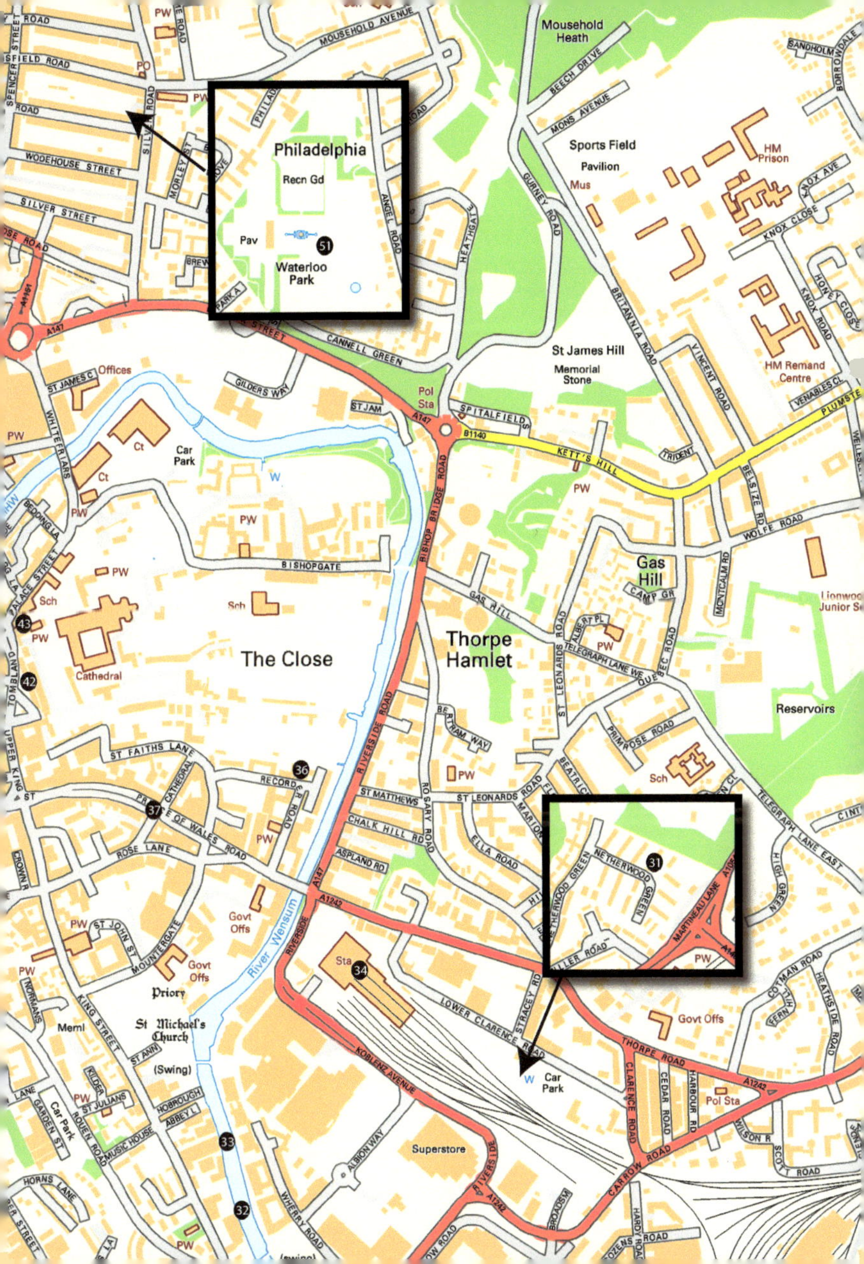

SPENCER STREET
ROAD
SFIELD ROAD
WODEHOUSE STREET
SILVER STREET
MORLEY ST
SILVER ROAD
PO
PW
MOUSEHOLD AVENUE
Mousehold Heath
BEECH DRIVE
MONS AVENUE
GURNEY ROAD
Sports Field
Pavilion
Mus
HM Prison
SANDHOLM
BORROWDALE
KNOX AVE
KNOX CLOSE
HONEY CLOSE
KNOX ROAD
HM Remand Centre
VENABLES CL
WELLS
PLUMSTE
WOLFE ROAD
Philadelphia
Recn Gd
Pav
Waterloo Park
51
PHILADE
ANGEL ROAD
HEATHGATE
CANNELL GREEN
ST JAM
A147
Pol Sta
SPITALFIELDS
B1140
KETT'S HILL
St James Hill
Memorial Stone
BRITANNIA ROAD
VINCENT ROAD
TRIDENT
BELSIZE RD
PW
Gas Hill
CAMP GR
MONTCALM RD
Lionwood Junior S
A147
GILDERS WAY
ST JAM
Offices
St James C
WHITEFRIARS
PW
Ct
Ct
PW
Car Park
W
PW
PW
BISHOPGATE
Sch
PW
Sch
The Close
BISHOP BRIDGE ROAD
GAS HILL
ALBERT PL
ST LEONARDS ROAD
TELEGRAPH LANE WE
QUE BEC ROAD
Thorpe Hamlet
PW
Reservoirs
Sch
BEDDING LA
PALACE STREET
Sch
PW
43
Cathedral
42
TOMBLAND
UPPER KING ST
ST FAITHS LANE
RECORDER ROAD
36
CATHEDRAL
PRINCE OF WALES ROAD
37
ROSE LANE
PW
CROWN R
RIVERSIDE ROAD
BERTRAM WAY
PW
ST MATTHEWS
ST LEONARDS ROAD
ST MATTHEWS
CHALK HILL ROAD
ROSARY ROAD
ELLA ROAD
ASPLAND RD
A147
A1242
Govt Offs
River Wensum
PW
ST JOHN ST
MOUNTERGATE
Govt Offs
Priory
NORMANS
PW
Meml
St Michael's Church
ST ANN
(Swing)
KING STREET
KILDER
ST JULIANS
PW
HOBROUGH
ABBEY L
33
MUSIC HOUSE
ROUEN ROAD
GARDEN ST
Car Park
HORNS LANE
LANE
32
WHERRY ROAD
KOBLENZ AVENUE
ALBION WAY
Superstore
RIVERSIDE
A1242
BROADSM
TOZENS ROAD
HARDY ROAD
Sta
34
LOWER CLARENCE ROAD
STRACEY RD
Car Park
W
THORPE ROAD
CLARENCE ROAD
CARROW ROAD
CEDAR ROAD
HARBOUR RD
WILSON R
SCOTT ROAD
A1242
Pol Sta
Govt Offs
FERN
HEATHSIDE ROAD
COTMAN ROAD
HIGH
SHERWOOD GREEN
NETHERWOOD GREEN
31
MARTINEAU LANE
BUTLER ROAD
HILL
PW
HIGH GREEN
TELEGRAPH LANE EAST
CINT
BEATRICE
MARION
PRIMROSE ROAD

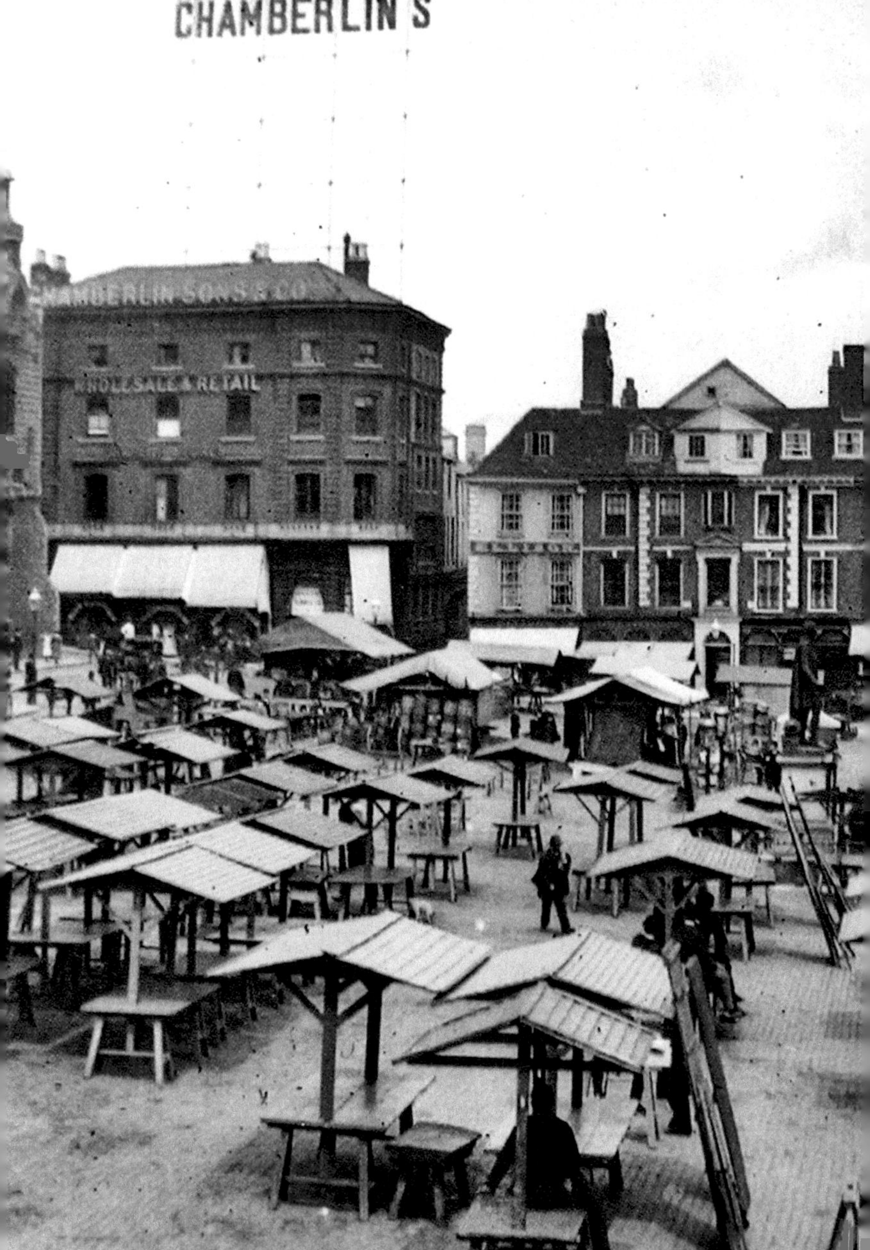

CHAMBERLIN'S
CHAMBERLIN SONS & CO
WHOLESALE & RETAIL

1. THE PROVISION MARKET

The market has been in broadly the same place since the Norman Conquest, but there were significant changes in the last century, and the stalls, which in the past were cleared away each weekend, first became permanent in 1938. The market has also expanded up the hill as Victorian buildings were swept away and the new City Hall was built.

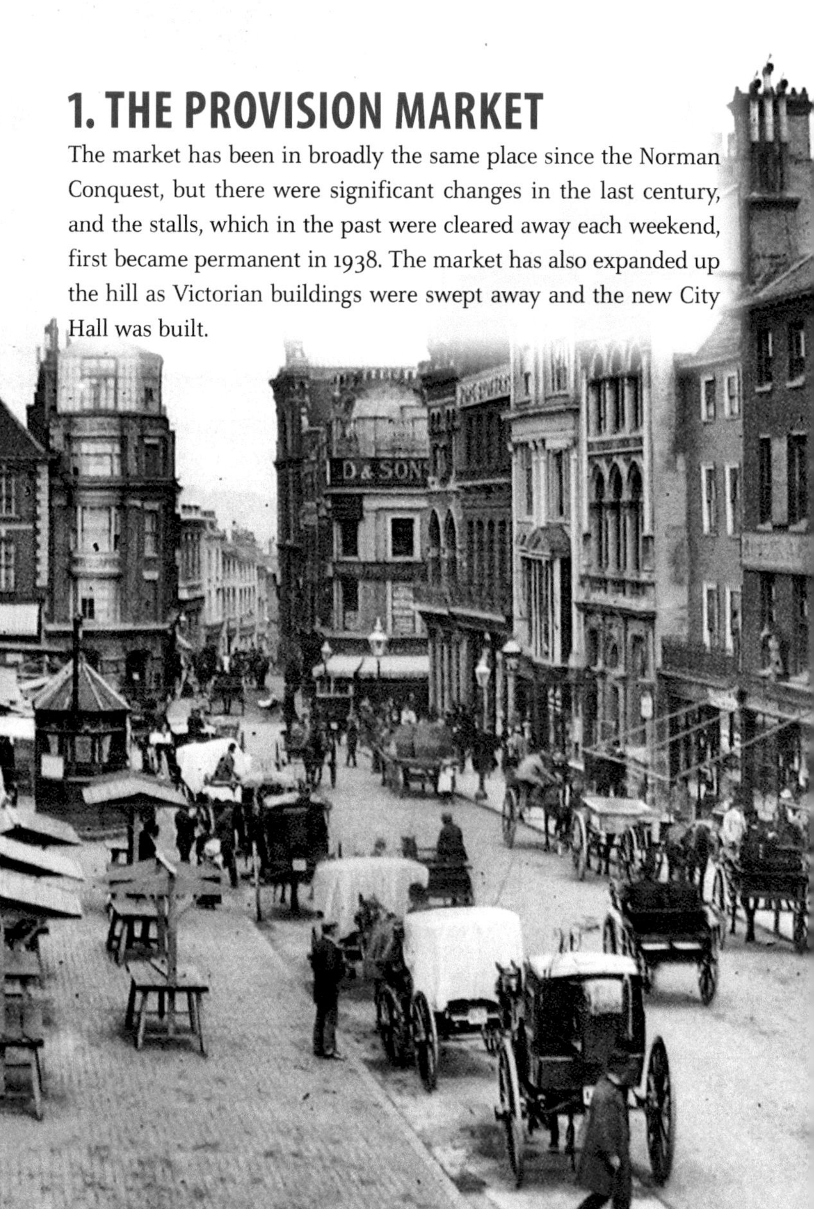

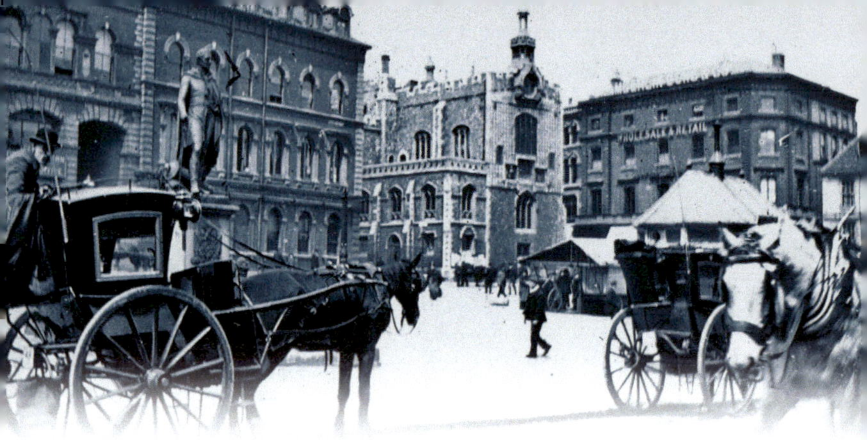

2. MARKET PLACE

Cabs wait in the Market Place, with the stalls cleared away. The statue is that of the Duke of Wellington, erected here in the Market Place in 1851. It was moved into the Cathedral Close in 1937, just before the opening of City Hall. Wellington can still be seen in the Close, opposite the more well-known statue of Admiral Nelson. Today, the stalls are permanent, and some open on Sundays.

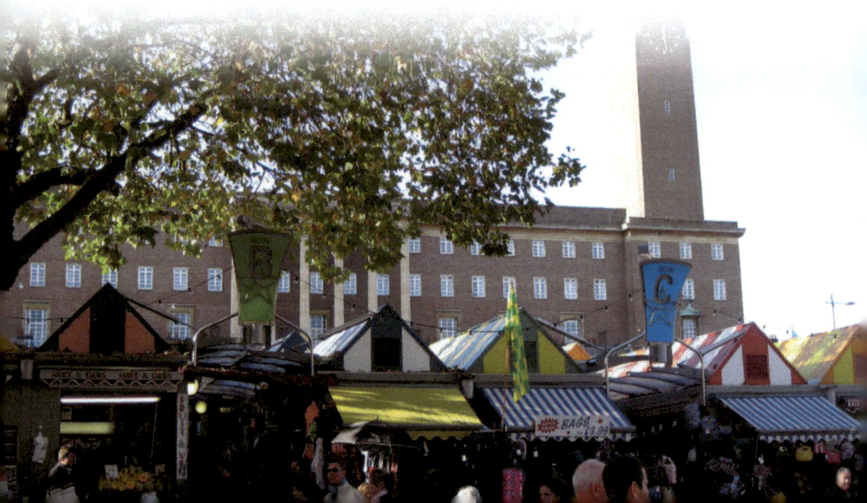

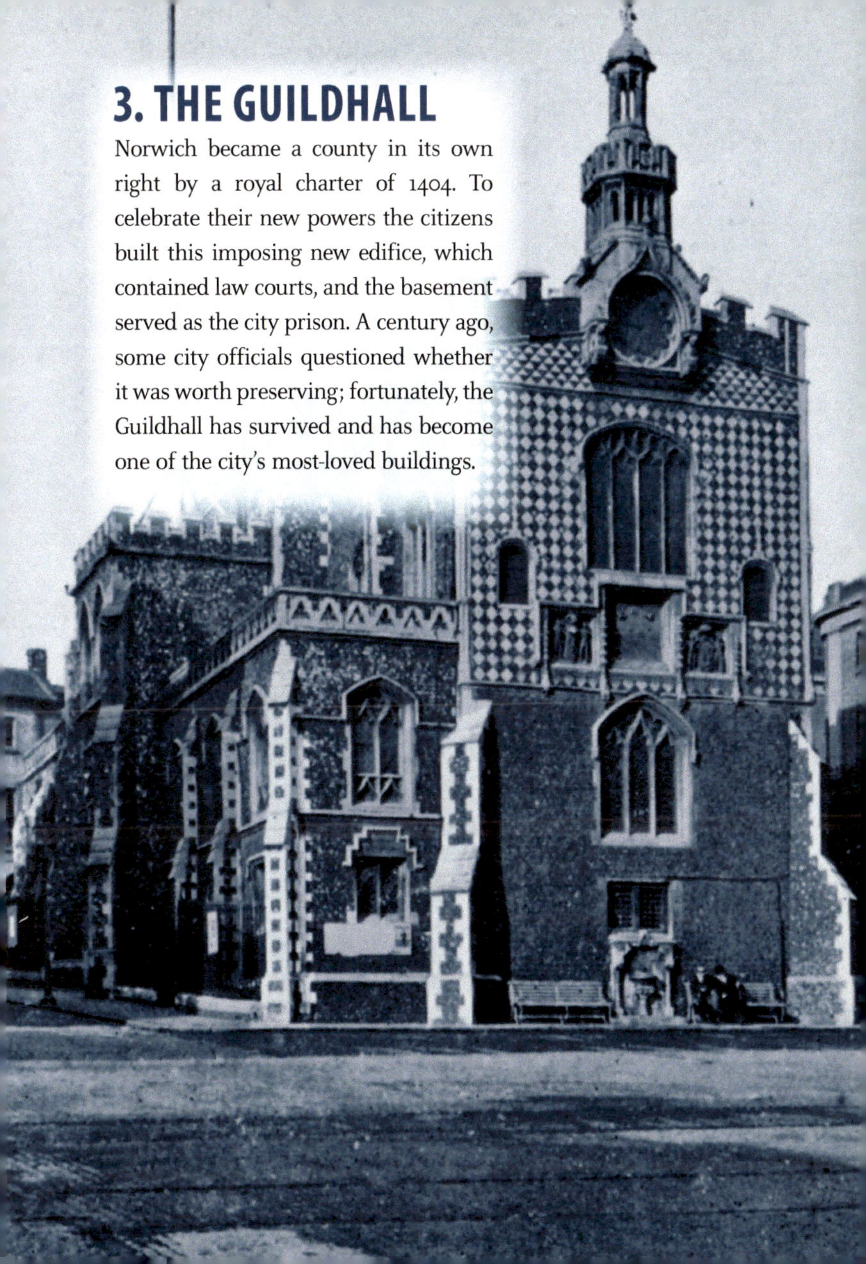

3. THE GUILDHALL

Norwich became a county in its own right by a royal charter of 1404. To celebrate their new powers the citizens built this imposing new edifice, which contained law courts, and the basement served as the city prison. A century ago, some city officials questioned whether it was worth preserving; fortunately, the Guildhall has survived and has become one of the city's most-loved buildings.

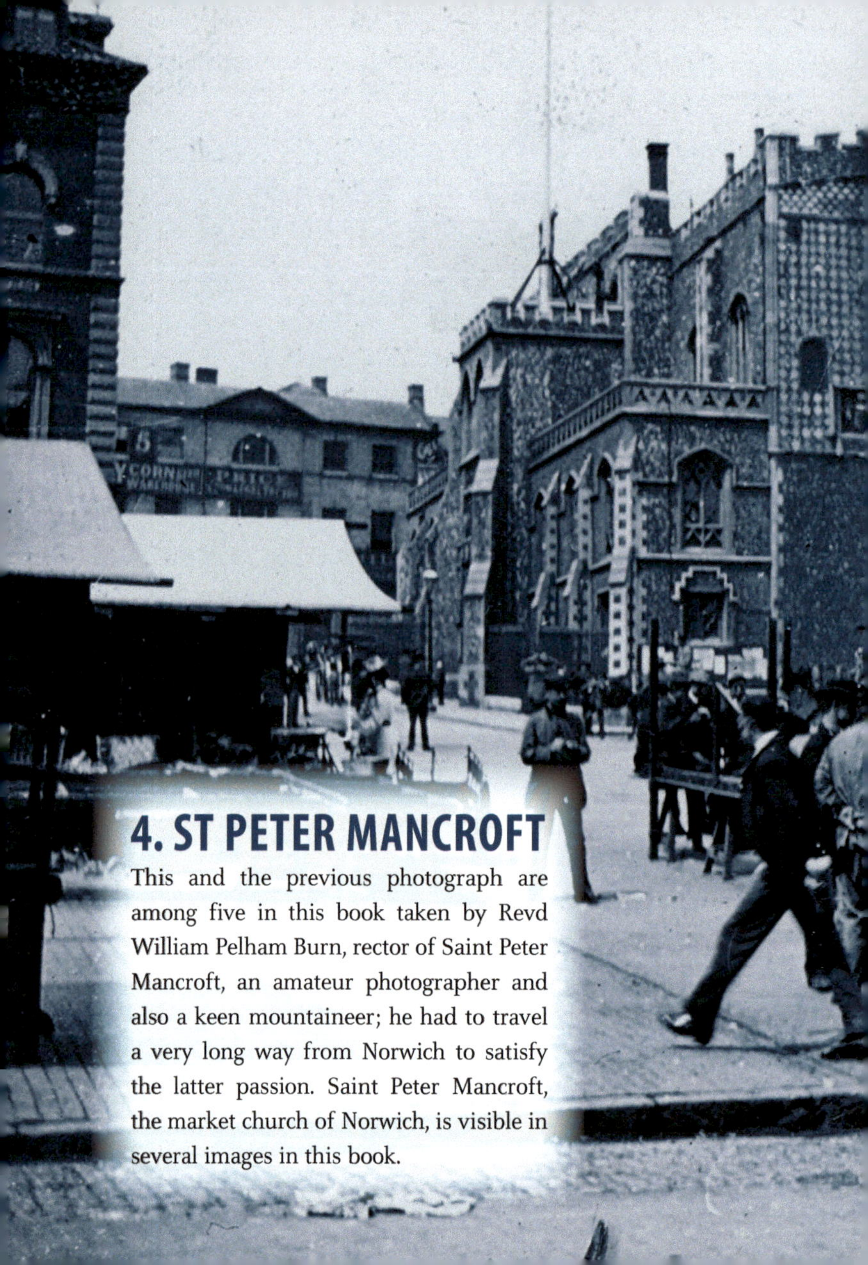

4. ST PETER MANCROFT

This and the previous photograph are among five in this book taken by Revd William Pelham Burn, rector of Saint Peter Mancroft, an amateur photographer and also a keen mountaineer; he had to travel a very long way from Norwich to satisfy the latter passion. Saint Peter Mancroft, the market church of Norwich, is visible in several images in this book.

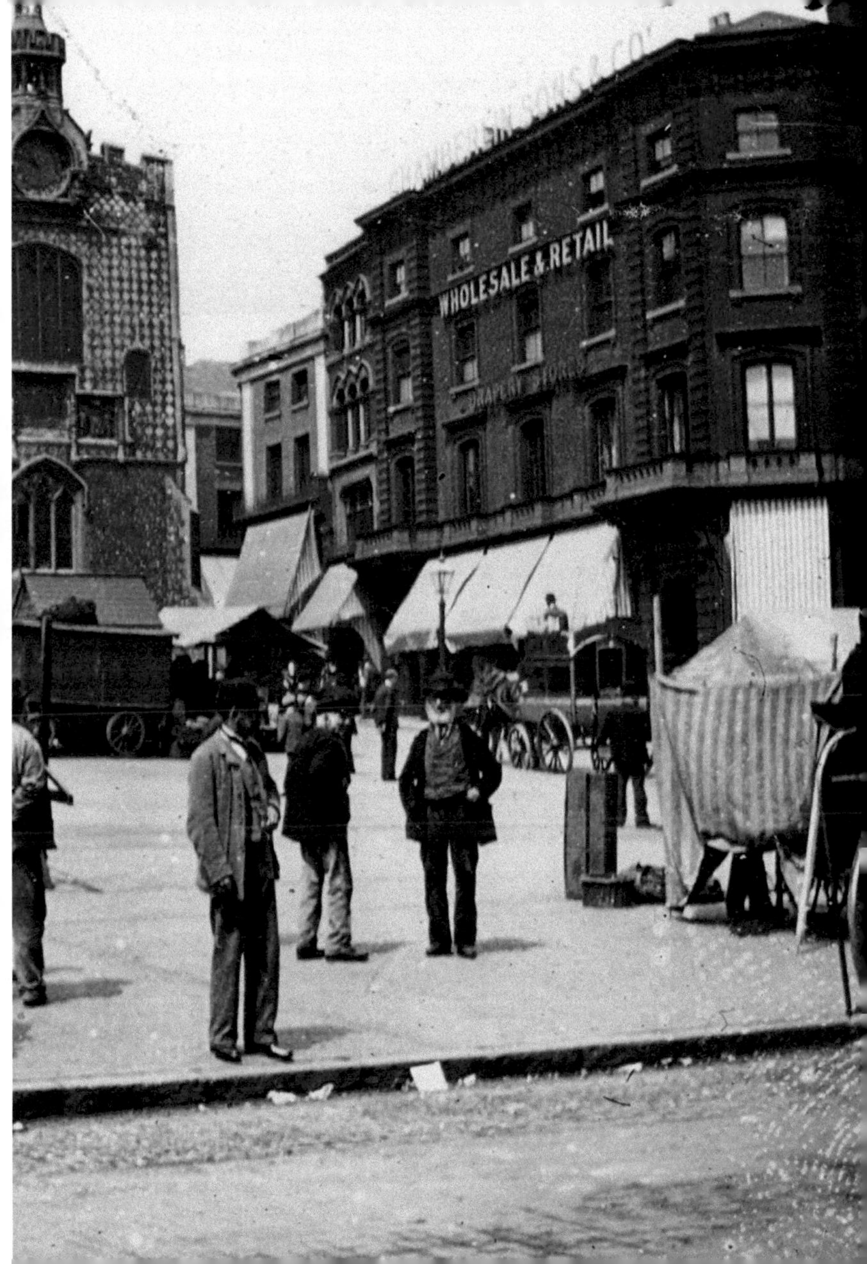
WHOLESALE & RETAIL
DRAPERY STORES

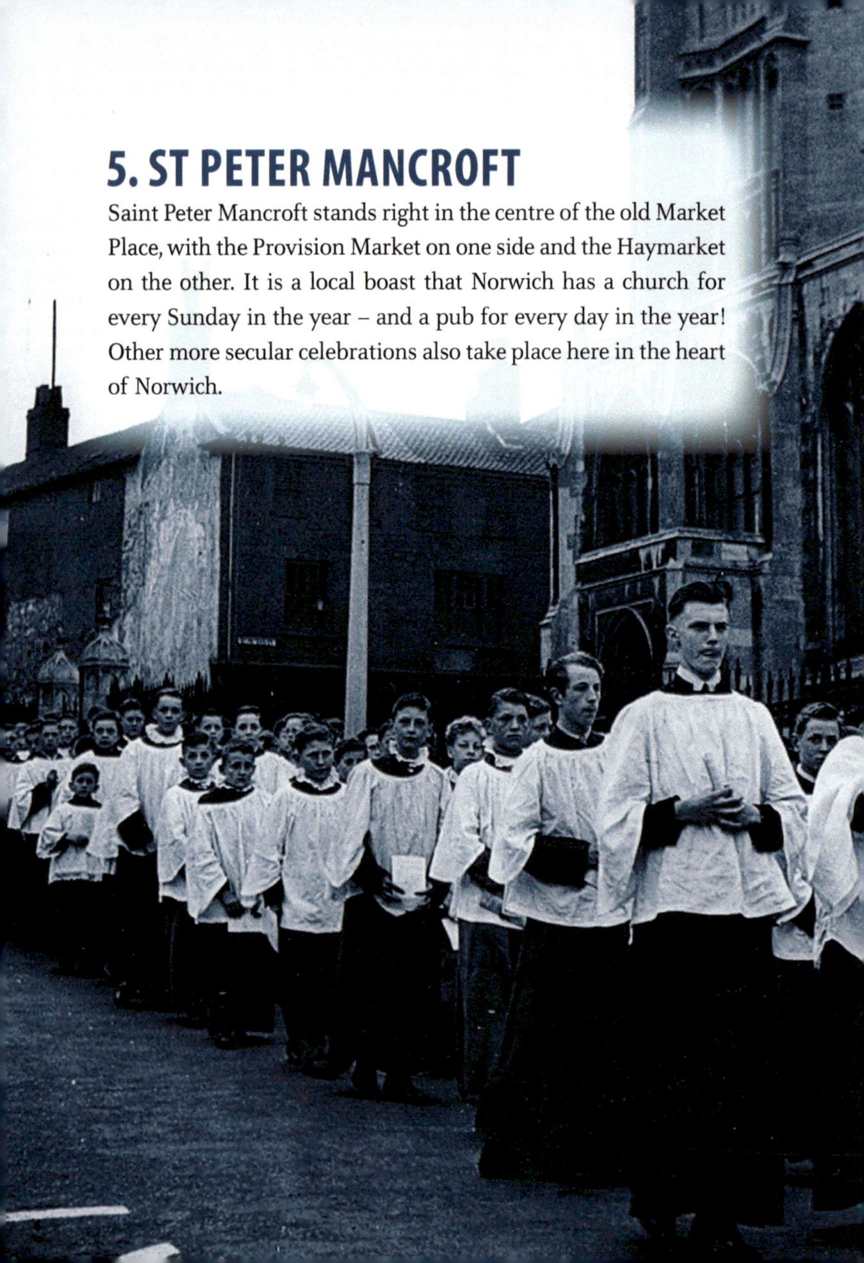

5. ST PETER MANCROFT

Saint Peter Mancroft stands right in the centre of the old Market Place, with the Provision Market on one side and the Haymarket on the other. It is a local boast that Norwich has a church for every Sunday in the year – and a pub for every day in the year! Other more secular celebrations also take place here in the heart of Norwich.

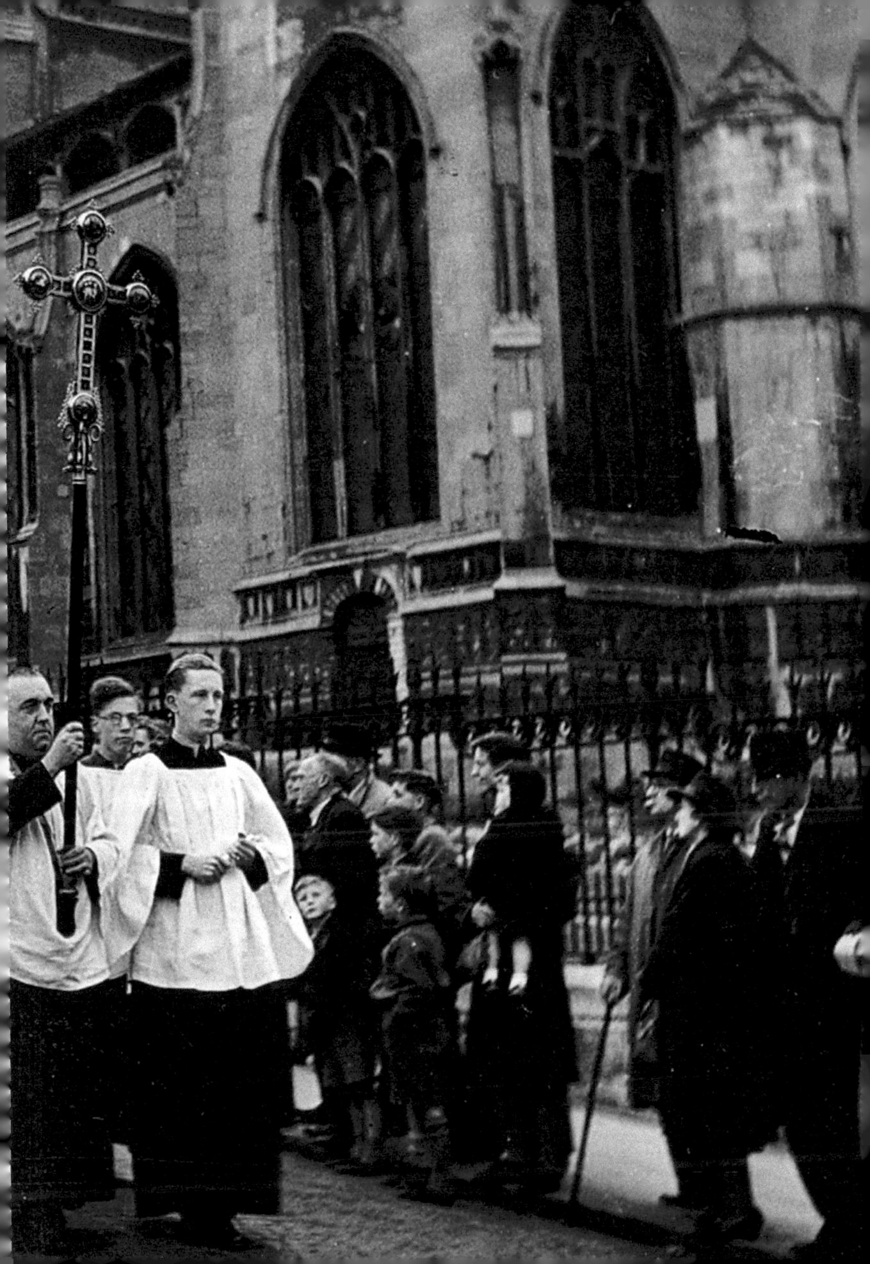

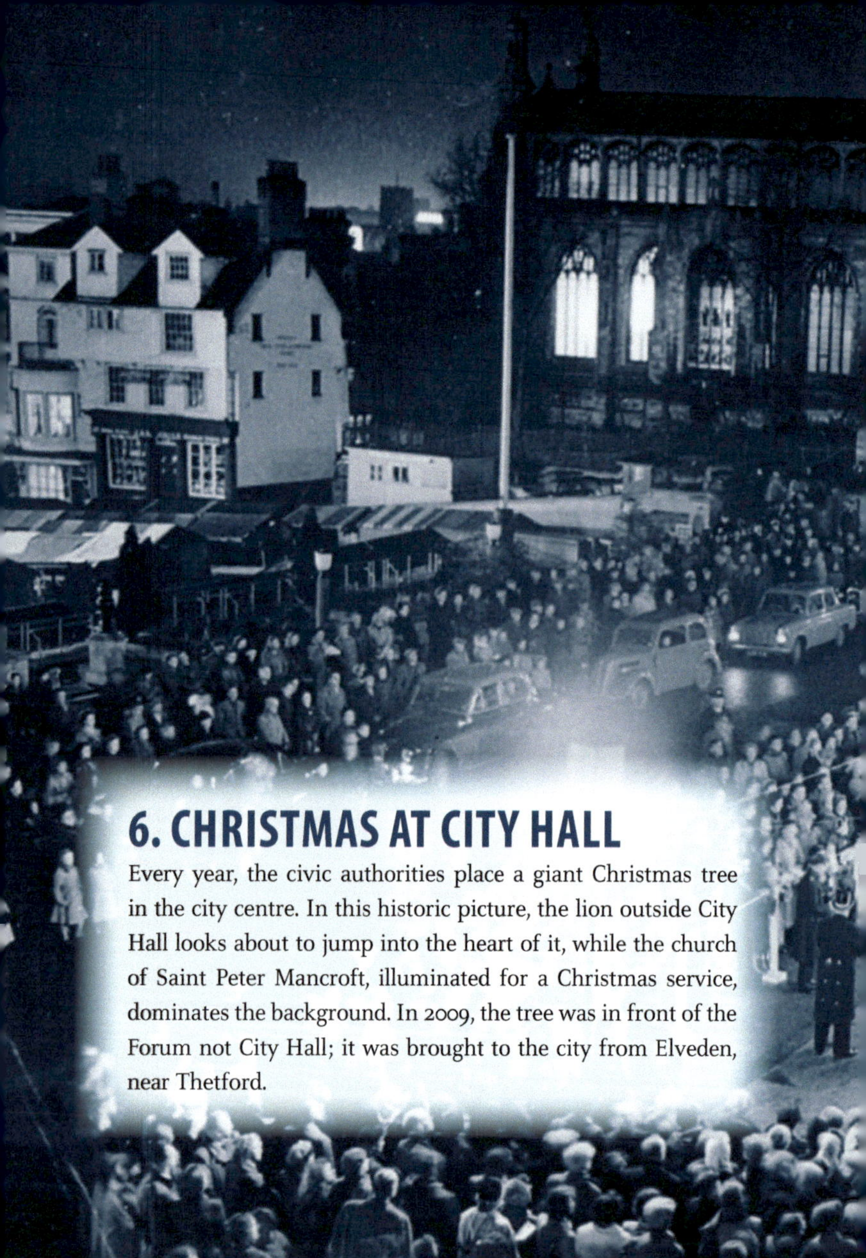

6. CHRISTMAS AT CITY HALL

Every year, the civic authorities place a giant Christmas tree in the city centre. In this historic picture, the lion outside City Hall looks about to jump into the heart of it, while the church of Saint Peter Mancroft, illuminated for a Christmas service, dominates the background. In 2009, the tree was in front of the Forum not City Hall; it was brought to the city from Elveden, near Thetford.

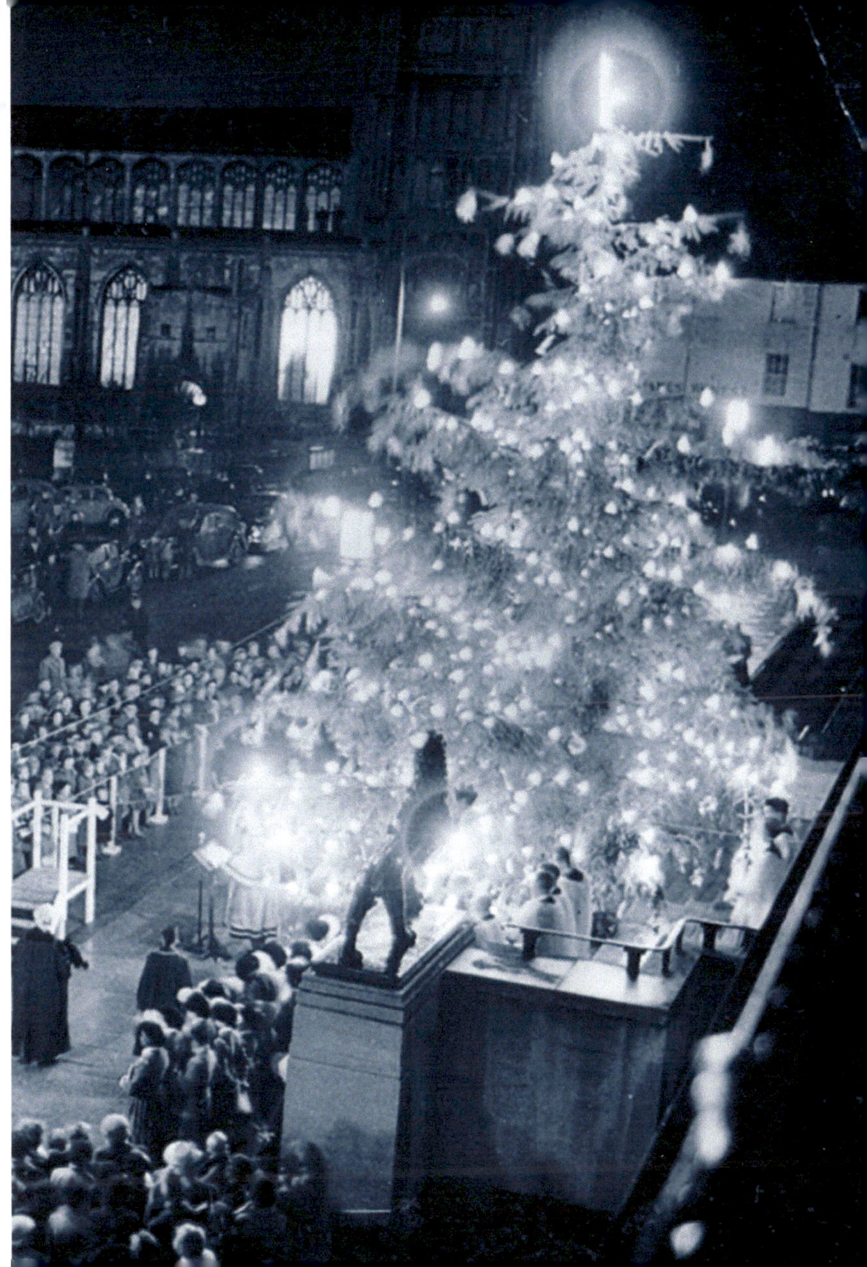

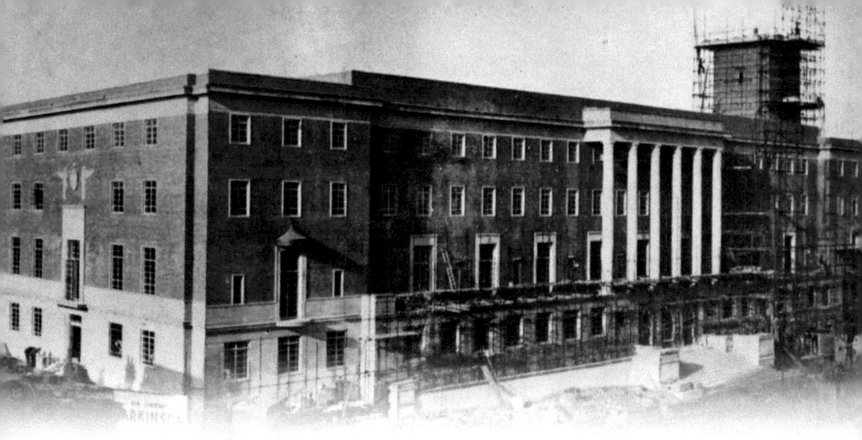

7. CITY HALL

Norwich's City Hall was a long time coming: it was planned at the beginning of the twentieth century but not finally built until the 1930s. The tower gives it its character, but was almost left un-built! Like all buildings of its kind, City Hall ran vastly over budget, and it was proposed to save money by omitting the tower; a large angel figure planned to surmount the tower *was* abandoned.

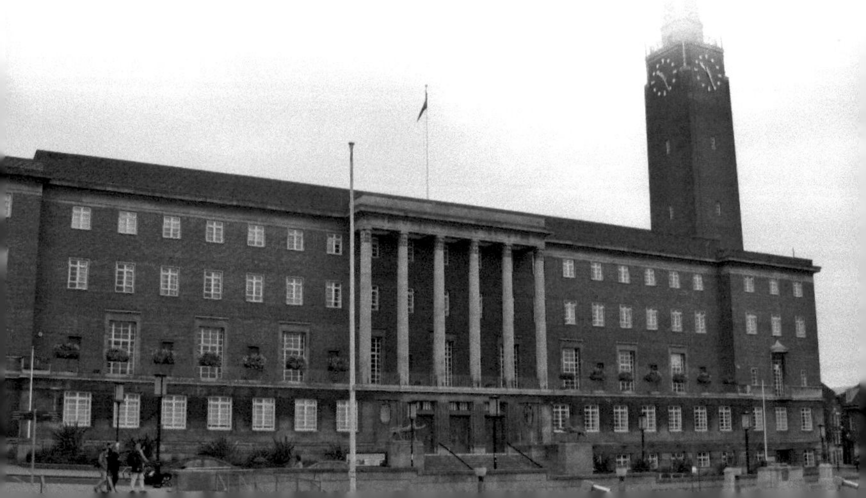

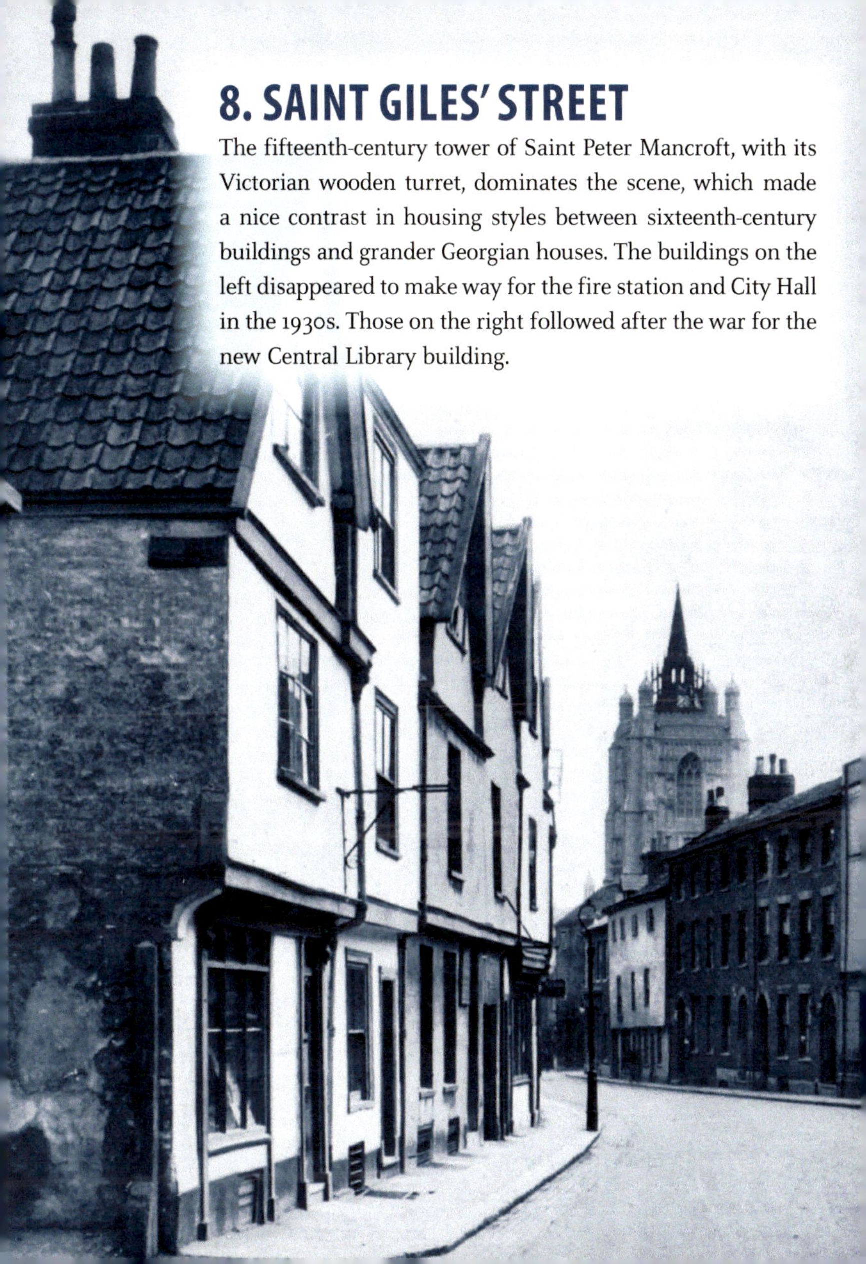

8. SAINT GILES' STREET

The fifteenth-century tower of Saint Peter Mancroft, with its Victorian wooden turret, dominates the scene, which made a nice contrast in housing styles between sixteenth-century buildings and grander Georgian houses. The buildings on the left disappeared to make way for the fire station and City Hall in the 1930s. Those on the right followed after the war for the new Central Library building.

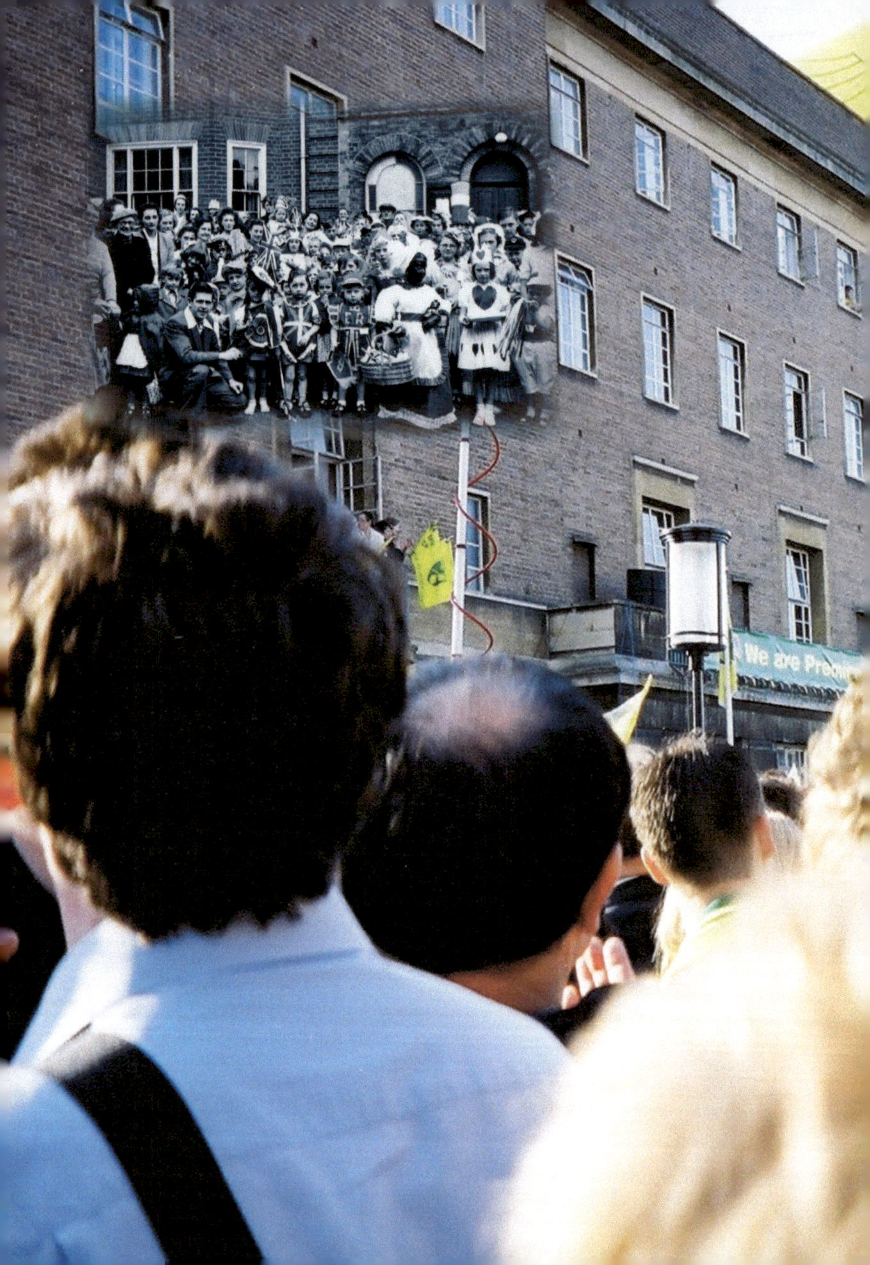
We are Prem

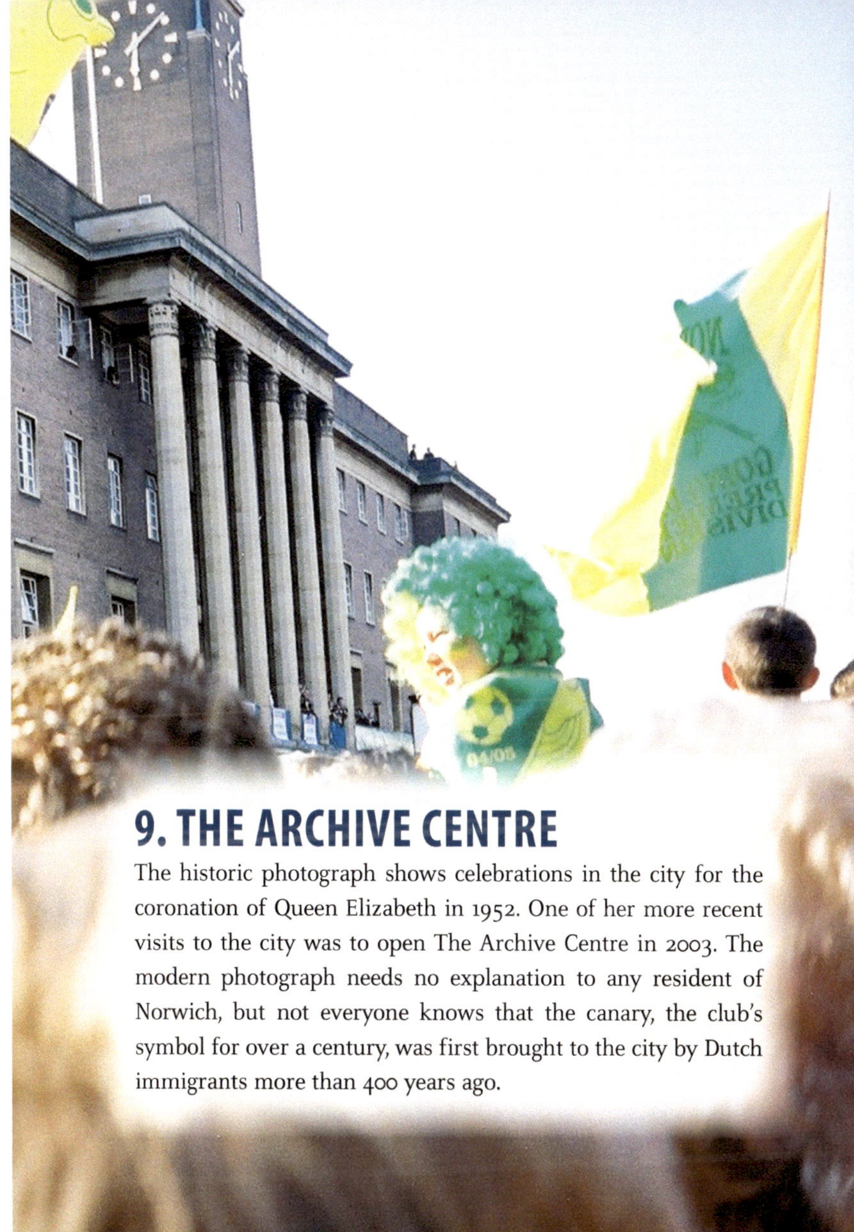

9. THE ARCHIVE CENTRE

The historic photograph shows celebrations in the city for the coronation of Queen Elizabeth in 1952. One of her more recent visits to the city was to open The Archive Centre in 2003. The modern photograph needs no explanation to any resident of Norwich, but not everyone knows that the canary, the club's symbol for over a century, was first brought to the city by Dutch immigrants more than 400 years ago.

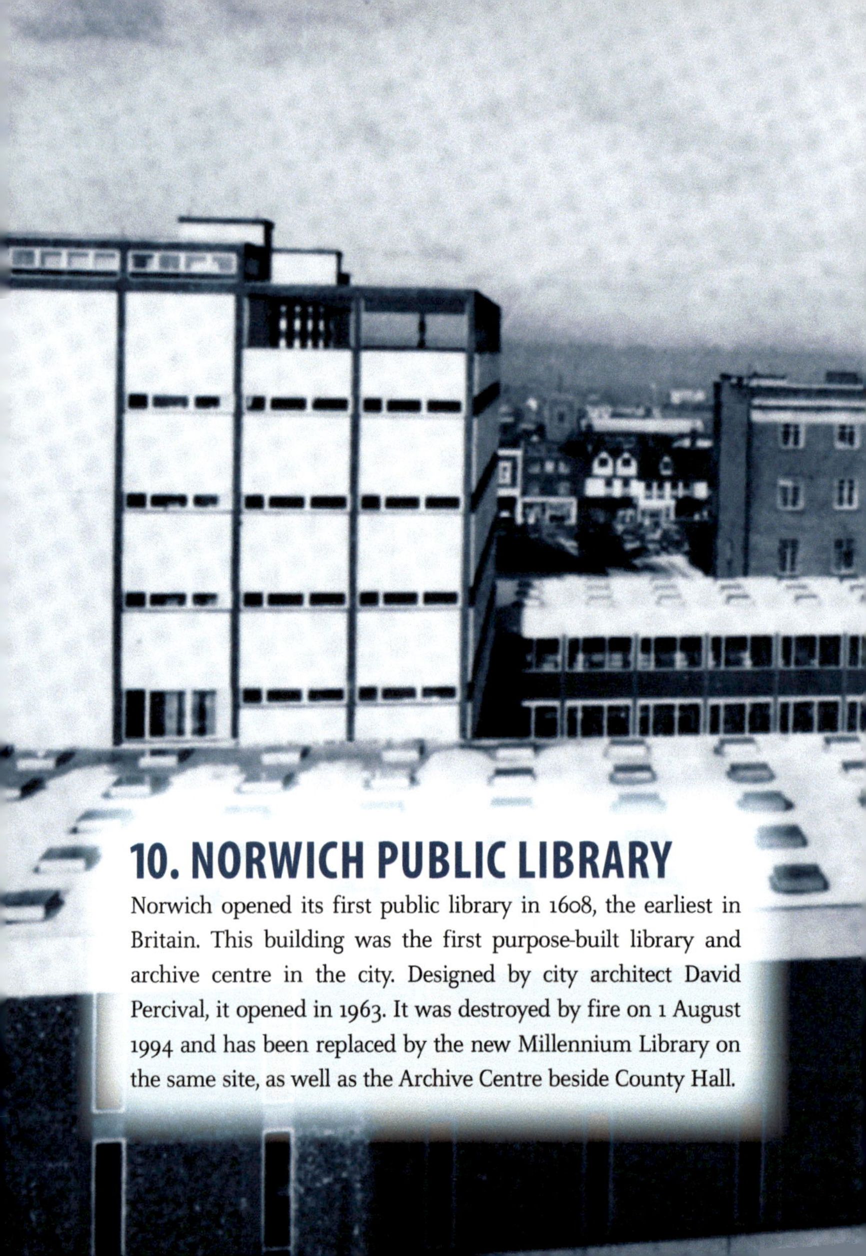

10. NORWICH PUBLIC LIBRARY

Norwich opened its first public library in 1608, the earliest in Britain. This building was the first purpose-built library and archive centre in the city. Designed by city architect David Percival, it opened in 1963. It was destroyed by fire on 1 August 1994 and has been replaced by the new Millennium Library on the same site, as well as the Archive Centre beside County Hall.

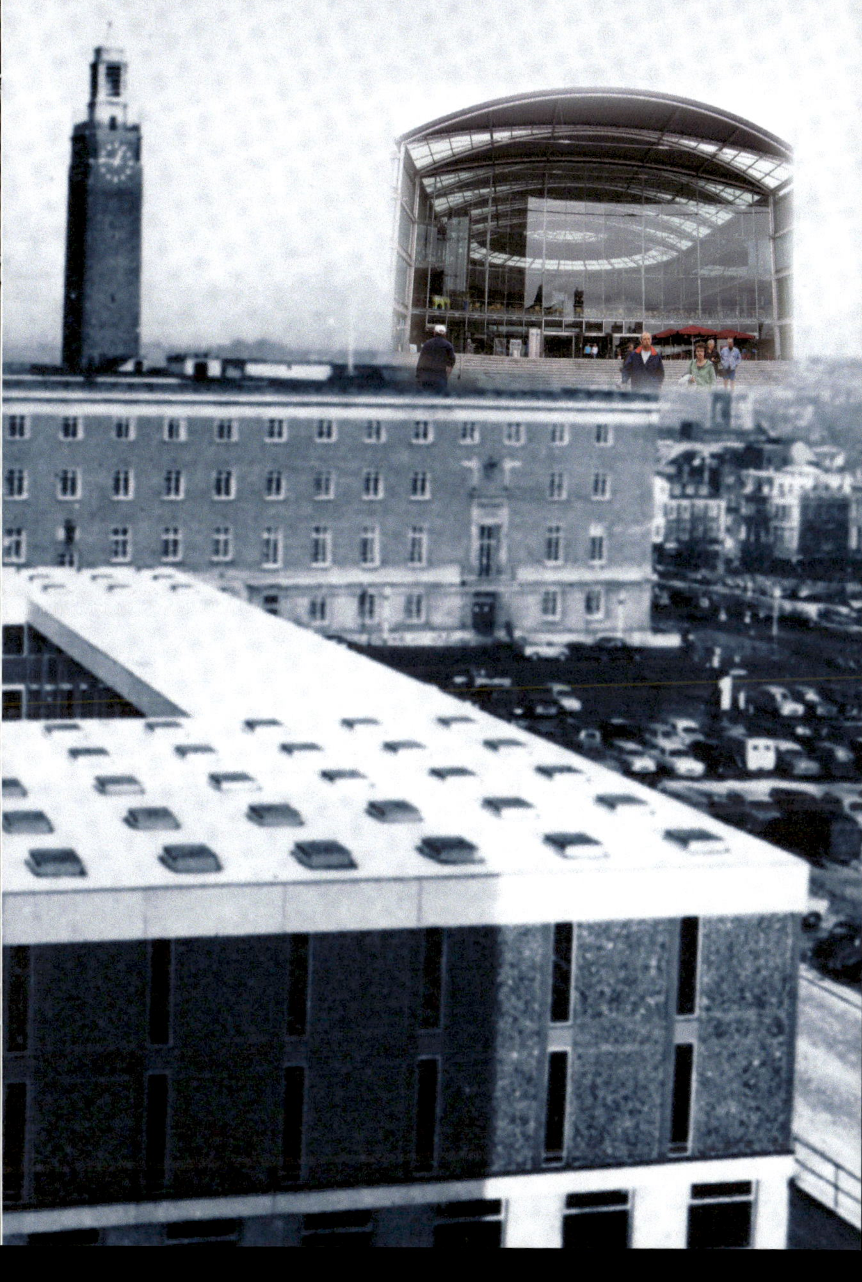

11. MARKET PLACE

Revd William Burn of Saint Peter Mancroft church was able to nip out of his place of work to photograph the celebration of Queen Victoria's diamond jubilee in the Market Place in 1897. Now that the stalls in the market are permanent, such occasions are limited to the smaller area outside City Hall.

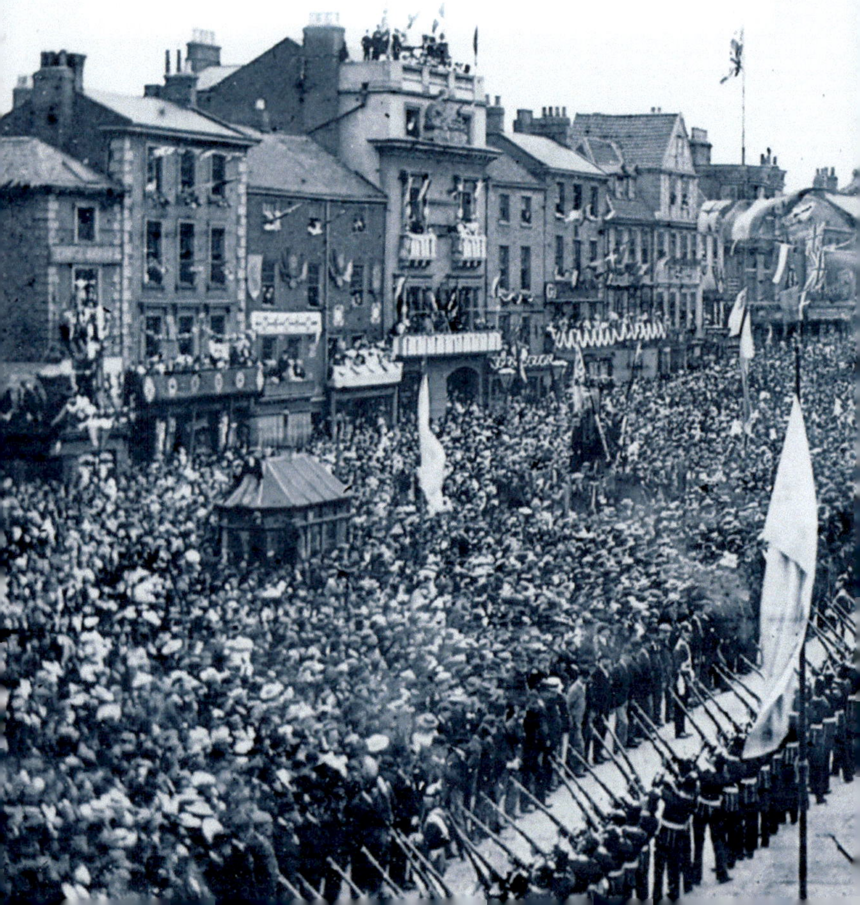

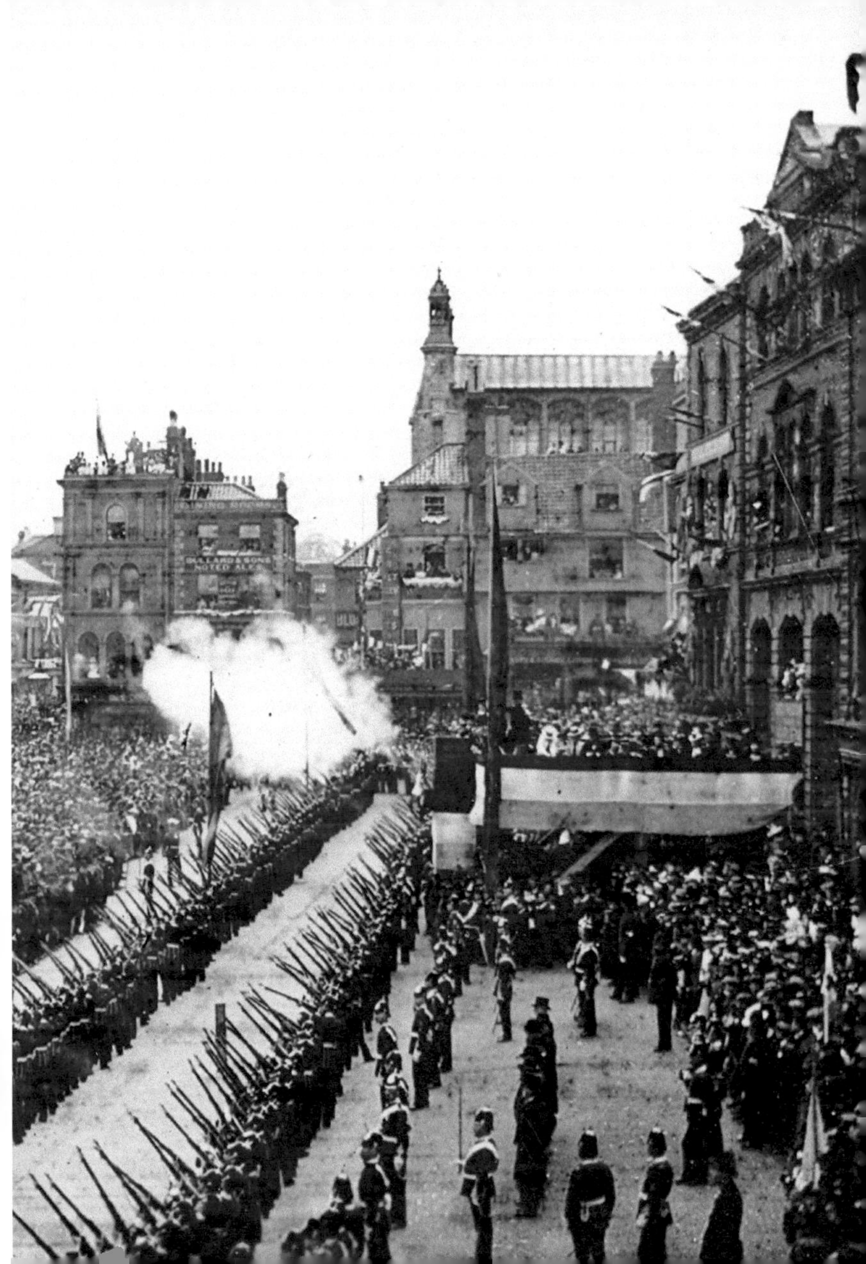

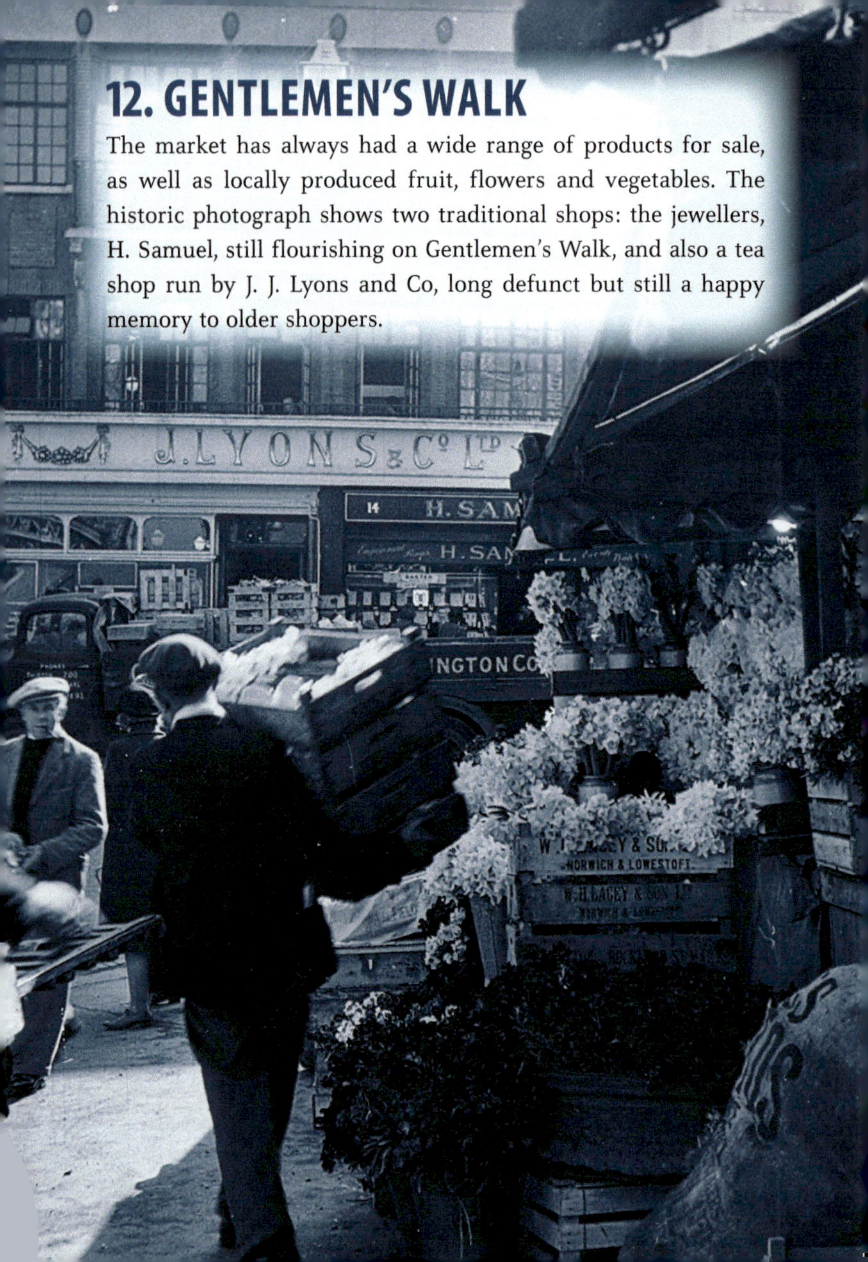

12. GENTLEMEN'S WALK

The market has always had a wide range of products for sale, as well as locally produced fruit, flowers and vegetables. The historic photograph shows two traditional shops: the jewellers, H. Samuel, still flourishing on Gentlemen's Walk, and also a tea shop run by J. J. Lyons and Co, long defunct but still a happy memory to older shoppers.

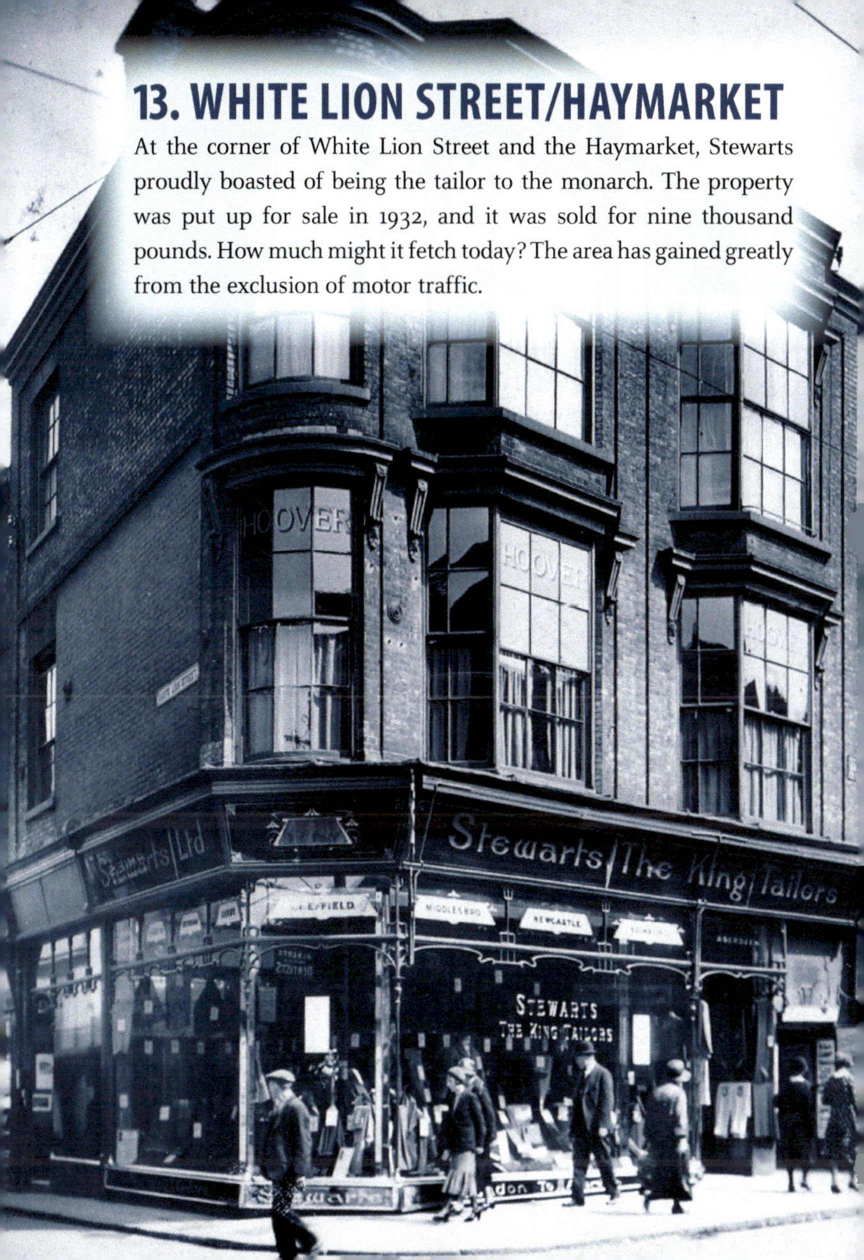

13. WHITE LION STREET/HAYMARKET

At the corner of White Lion Street and the Haymarket, Stewarts proudly boasted of being the tailor to the monarch. The property was put up for sale in 1932, and it was sold for nine thousand pounds. How much might it fetch today? The area has gained greatly from the exclusion of motor traffic.

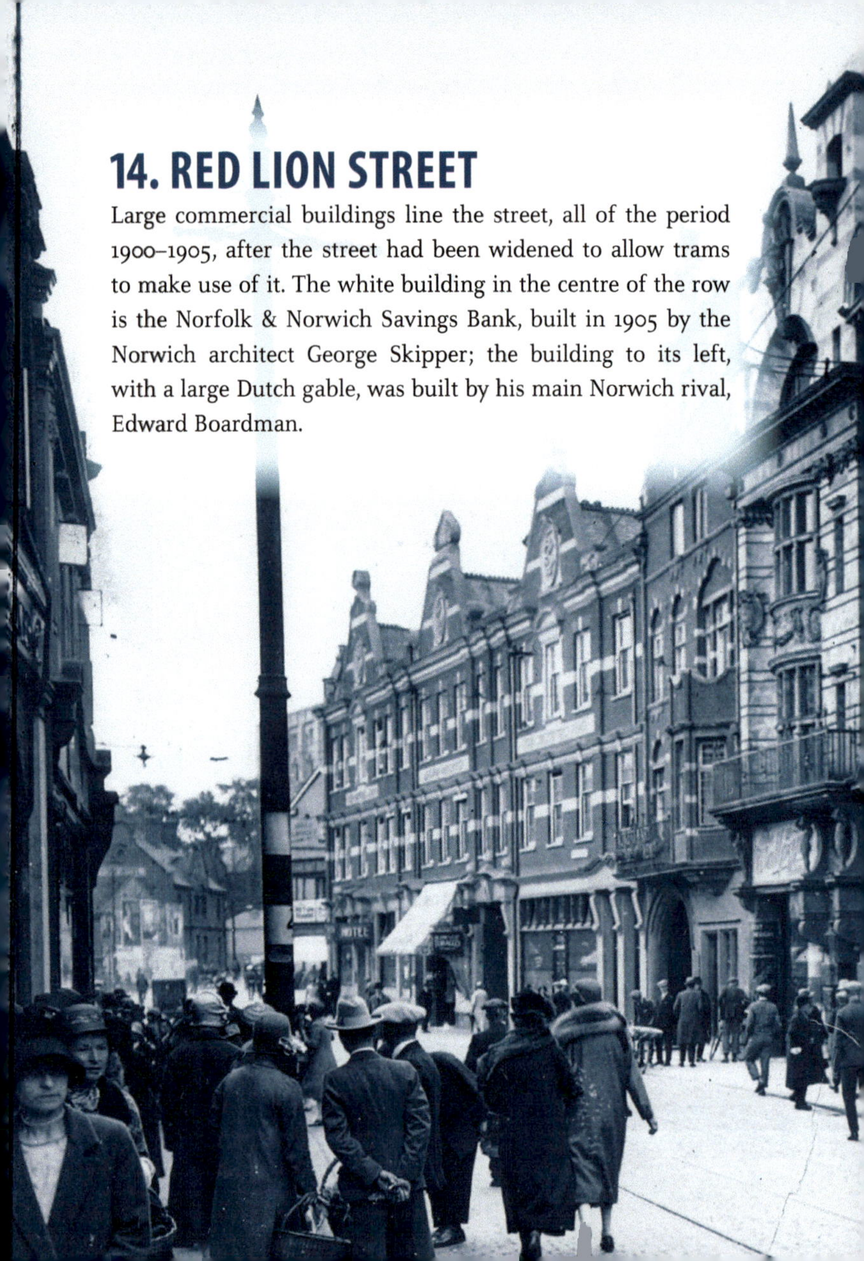

14. RED LION STREET

Large commercial buildings line the street, all of the period 1900–1905, after the street had been widened to allow trams to make use of it. The white building in the centre of the row is the Norfolk & Norwich Savings Bank, built in 1905 by the Norwich architect George Skipper; the building to its left, with a large Dutch gable, was built by his main Norwich rival, Edward Boardman.

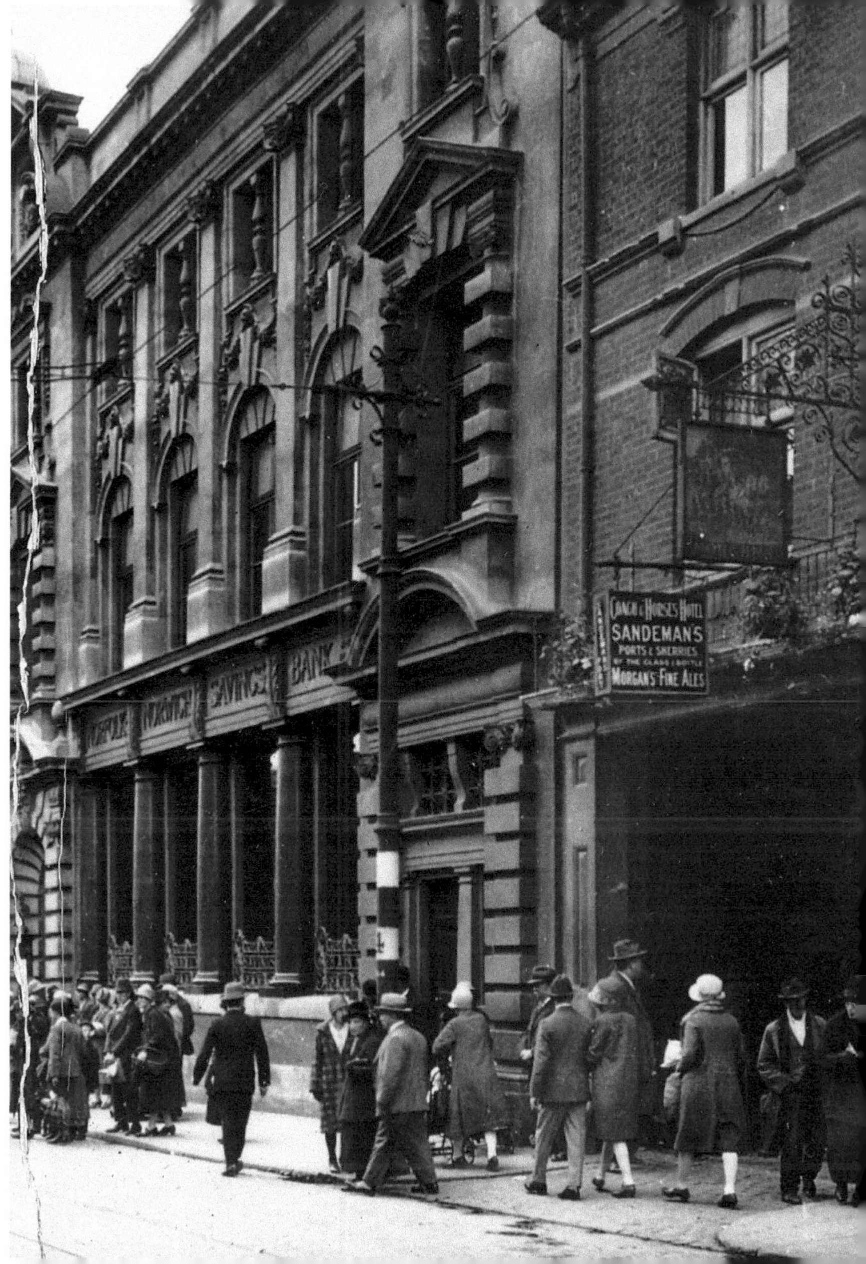
SAVINGS BANK
COACH & HORSES HOTEL
SANDEMANS
PORTS & SHERRIES
BY THE GLASS & BOTTLE
MORGAN'S FINE ALES

15. THE SAVINGS BANK

Norwich has been a centre for banking and insurance for well over two centuries, with farmers from the county bringing their savings into the city. This solid nineteenth-century savings bank building was pulled down in 1899, so that the corner could be widened for trams, which have themselves long disappeared; its early twentieth-century replacement has seen a wide range of uses.

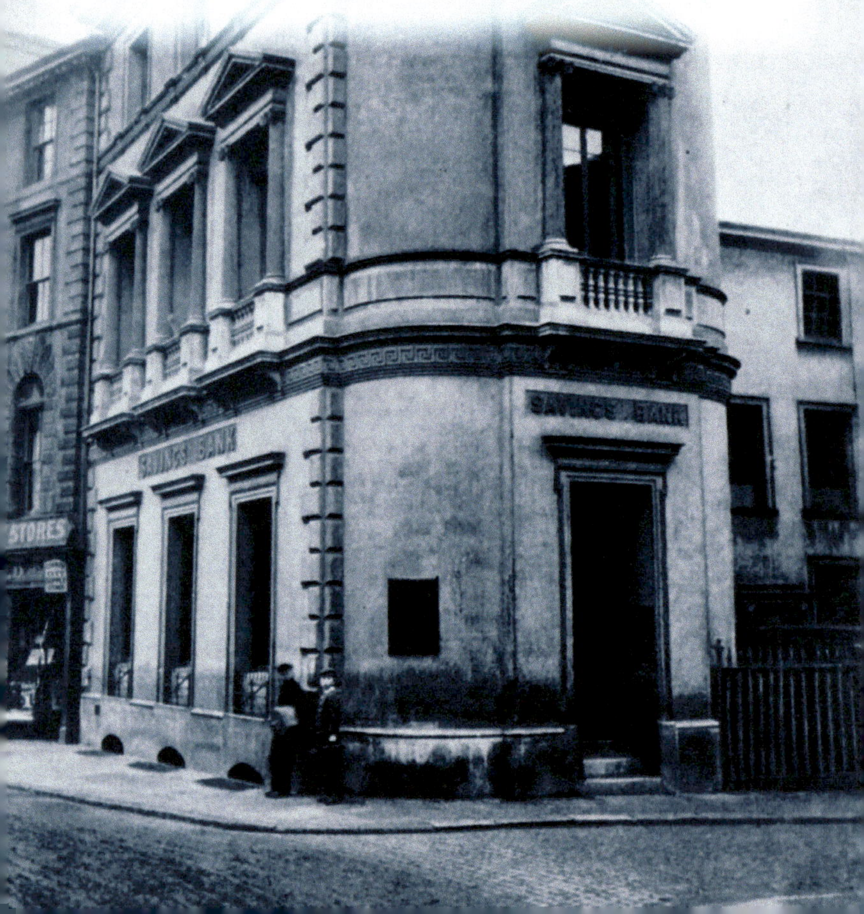

16. BUNTINGS CORNER

The junction of Rampant Horse Street, Westlegate, Red Lion Street and Saint Stephens has always been the heart of commercial Norwich. It was known as Buntings Corner after a store where Marks & Spencer now stands; a few of the older residents of the city still call it by this name. The historic photograph shows motor traffic, tramlines and evidence of horse traffic (the dark objects in the road). The scene is very different today, but the plan is to reduce the traffic flow at this spot.

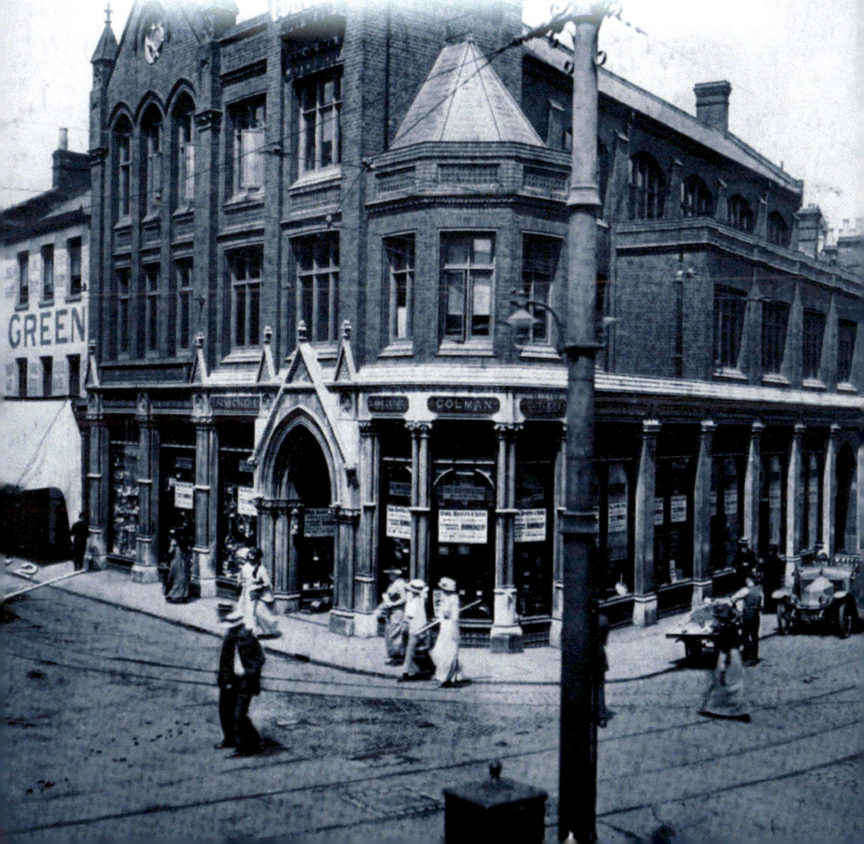

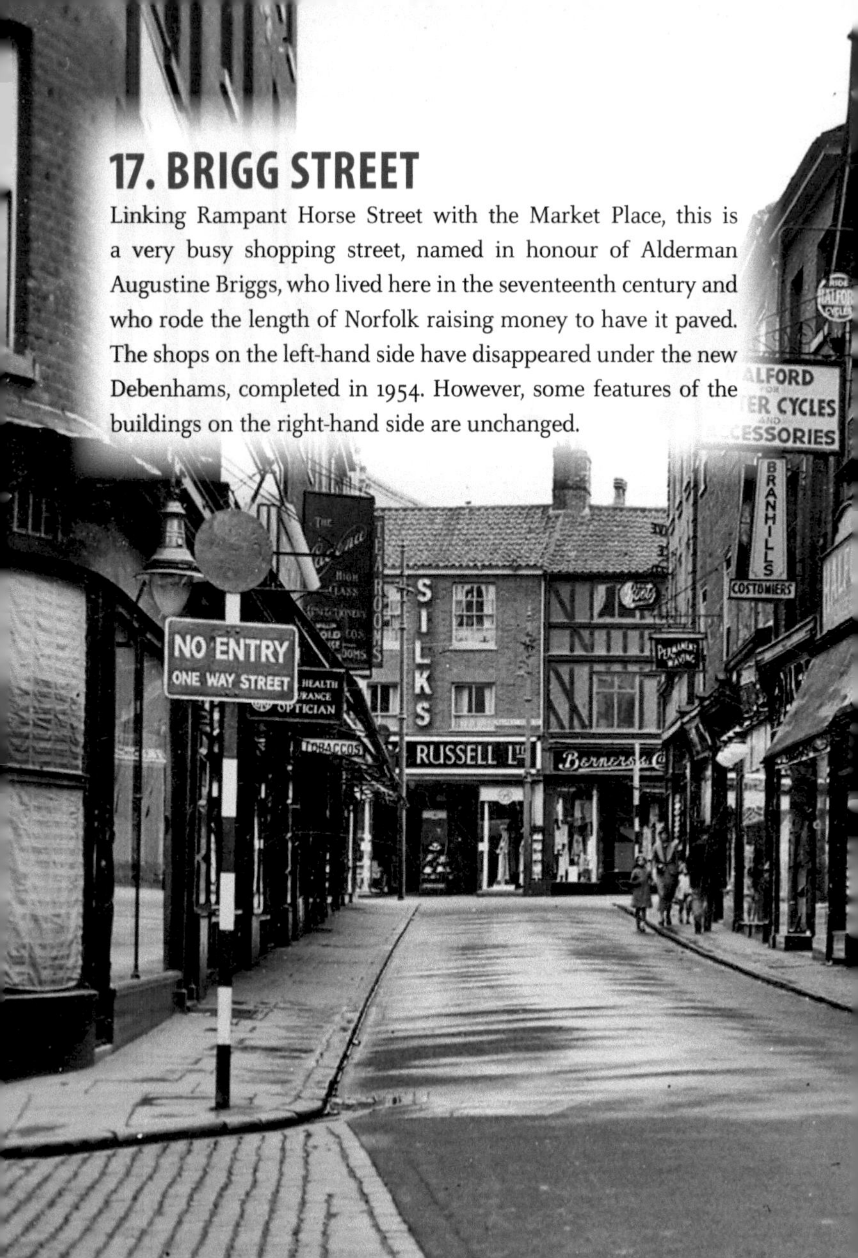

17. BRIGG STREET

Linking Rampant Horse Street with the Market Place, this is a very busy shopping street, named in honour of Alderman Augustine Briggs, who lived here in the seventeenth century and who rode the length of Norfolk raising money to have it paved. The shops on the left-hand side have disappeared under the new Debenhams, completed in 1954. However, some features of the buildings on the right-hand side are unchanged.

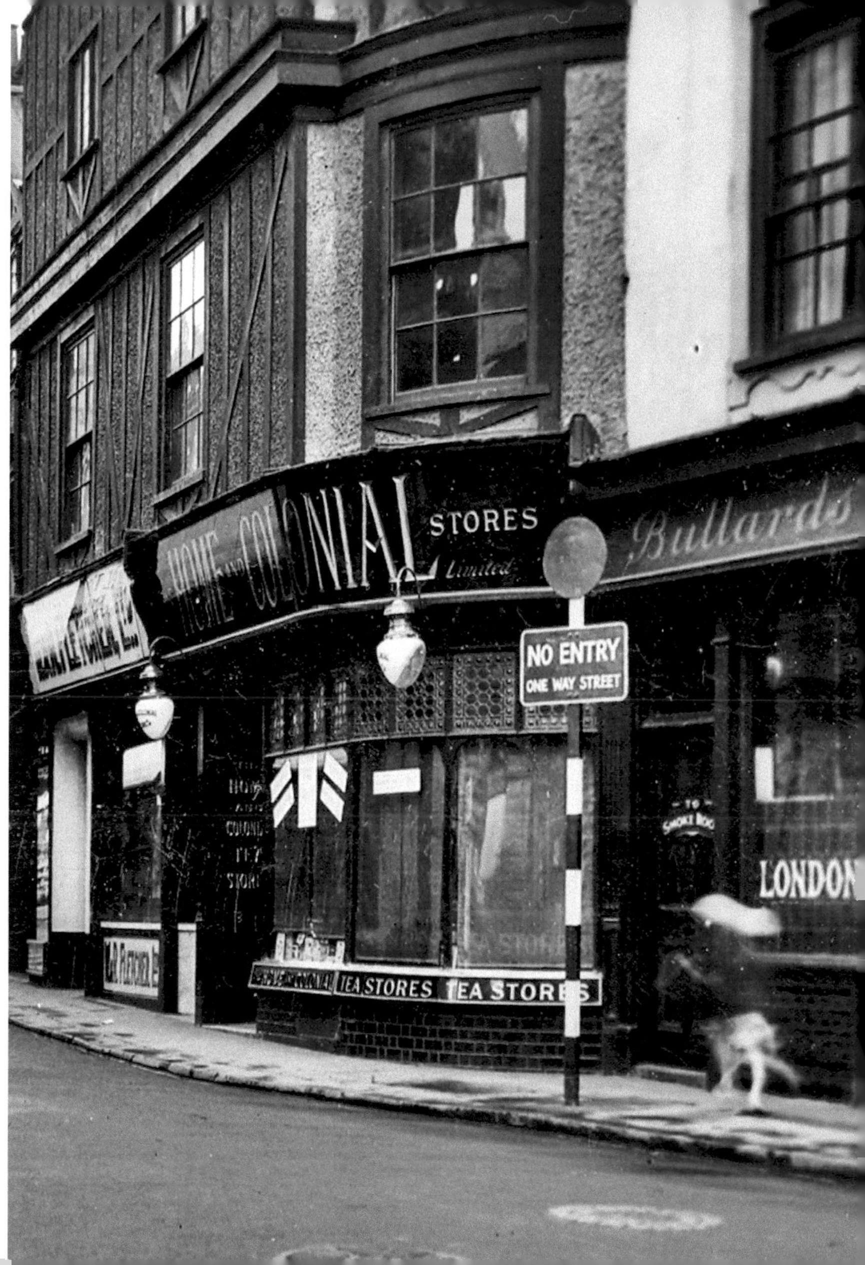

HOME AND COLONIAL STORES Limited
Bullards
NO ENTRY
ONE WAY STREET
HOME AND COLONIAL TEA STORES
TEA STORES TEA STORES
LONDON

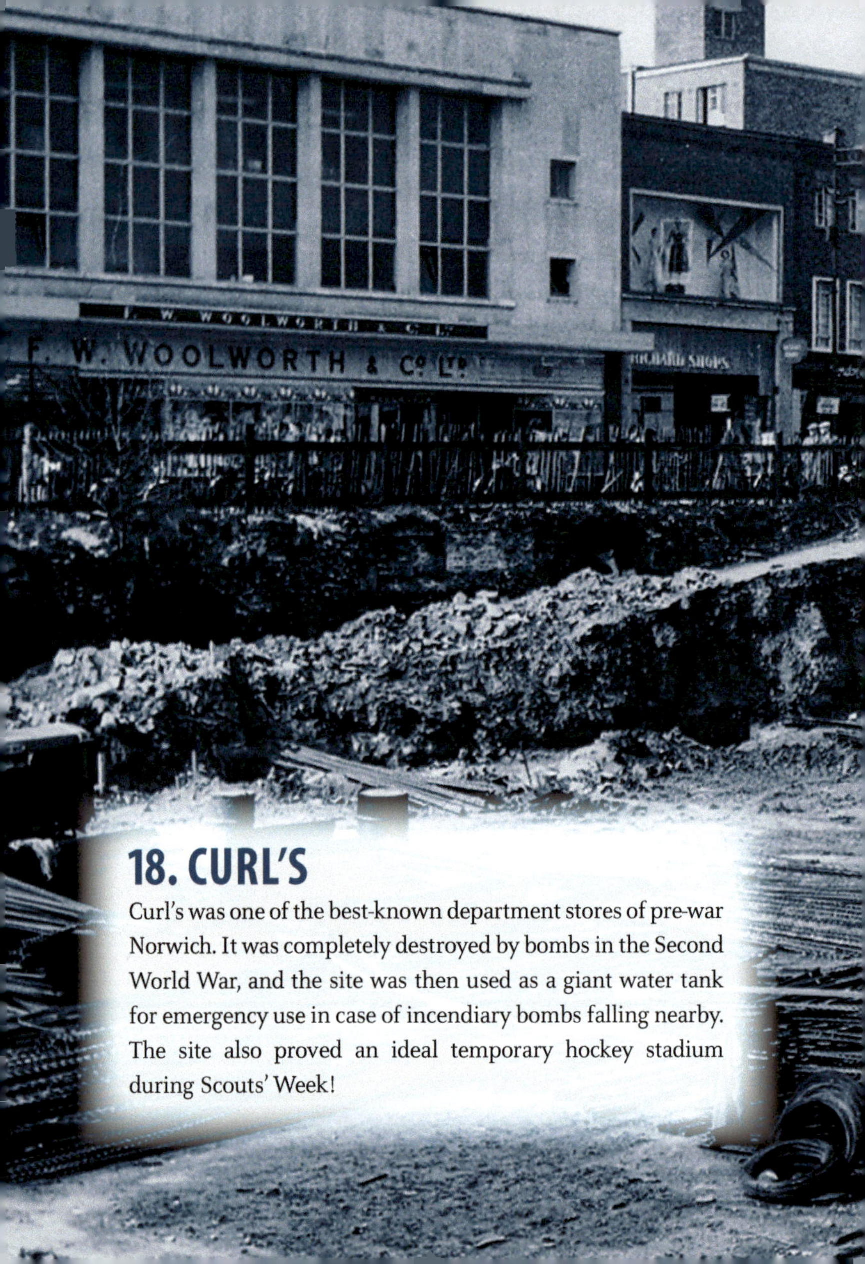

18. CURL'S

Curl's was one of the best-known department stores of pre-war Norwich. It was completely destroyed by bombs in the Second World War, and the site was then used as a giant water tank for emergency use in case of incendiary bombs falling nearby. The site also proved an ideal temporary hockey stadium during Scouts' Week!

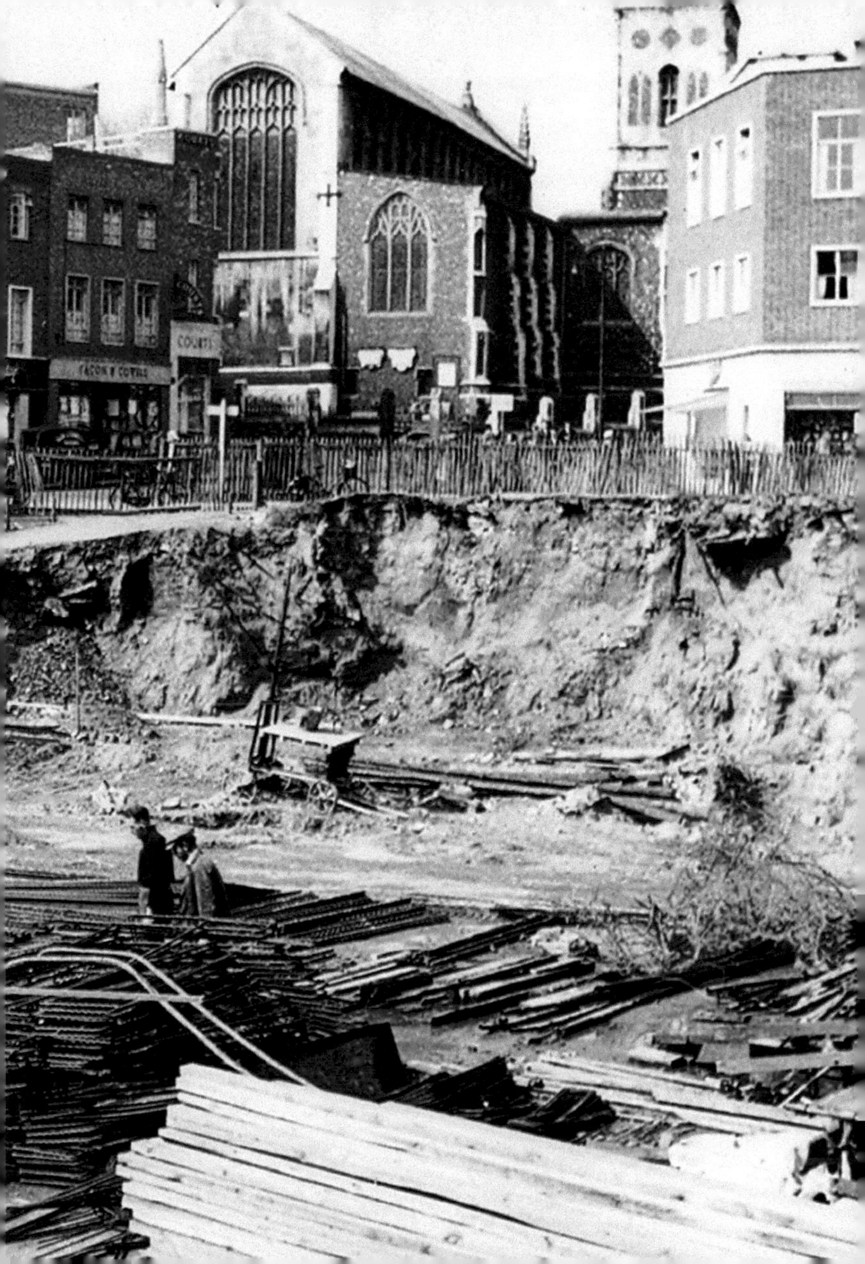

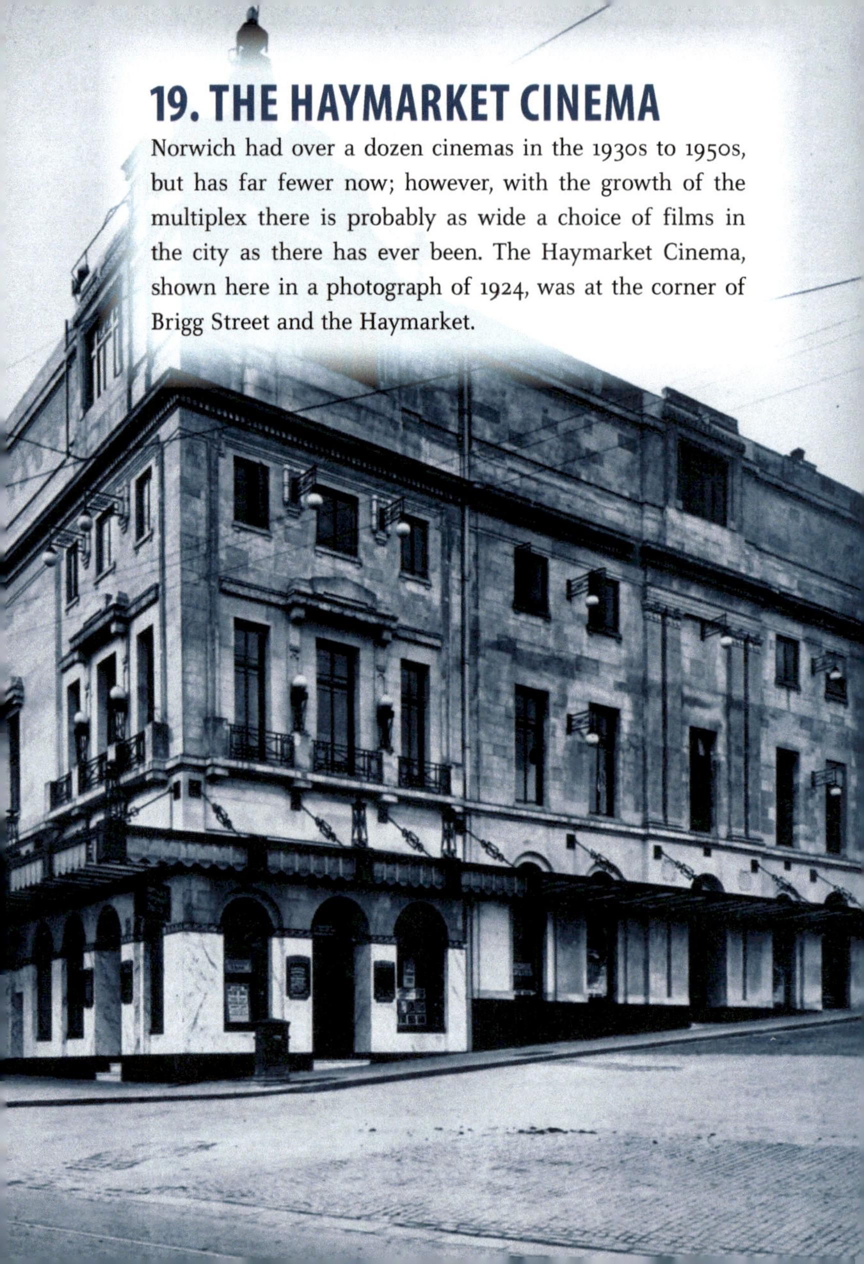

19. THE HAYMARKET CINEMA

Norwich had over a dozen cinemas in the 1930s to 1950s, but has far fewer now; however, with the growth of the multiplex there is probably as wide a choice of films in the city as there has ever been. The Haymarket Cinema, shown here in a photograph of 1924, was at the corner of Brigg Street and the Haymarket.

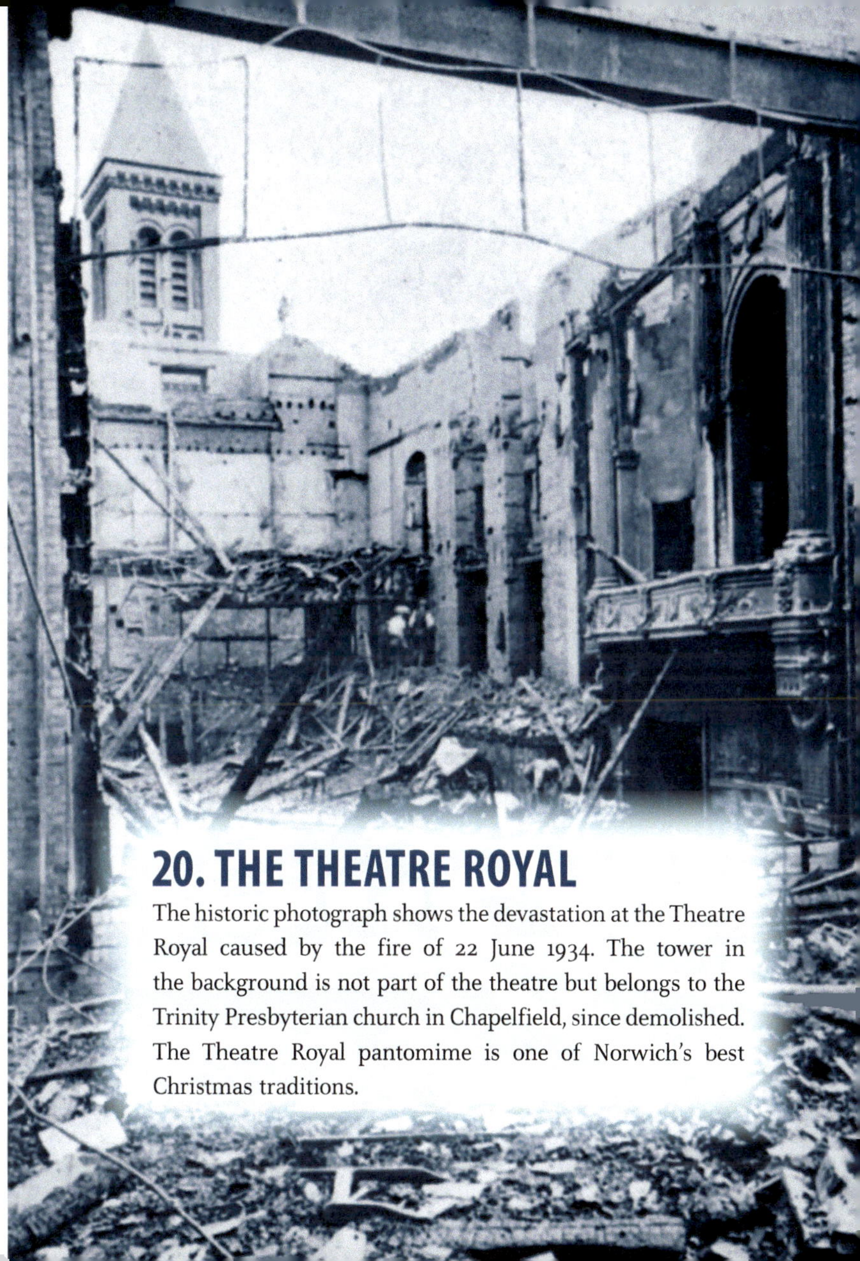

20. THE THEATRE ROYAL

The historic photograph shows the devastation at the Theatre Royal caused by the fire of 22 June 1934. The tower in the background is not part of the theatre but belongs to the Trinity Presbyterian church in Chapelfield, since demolished. The Theatre Royal pantomime is one of Norwich's best Christmas traditions.

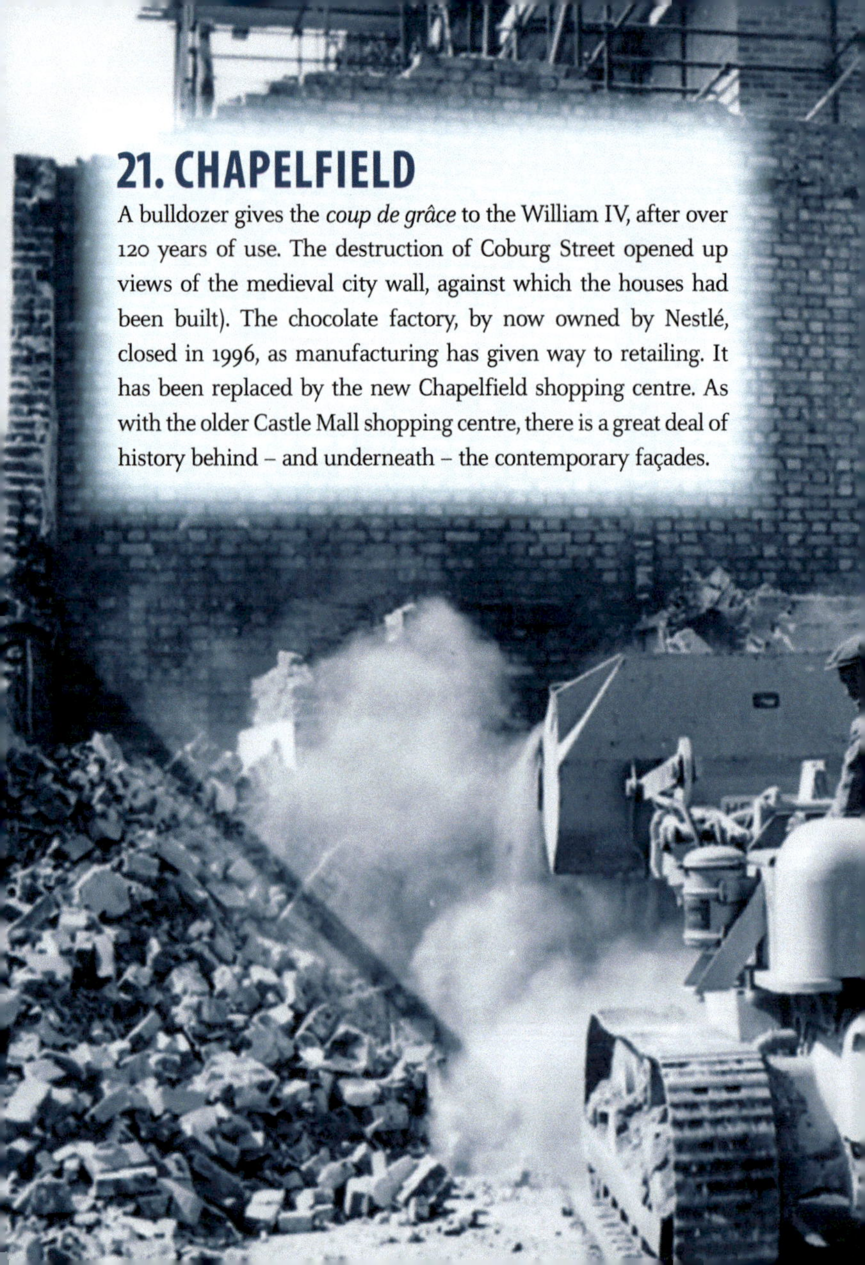

21. CHAPELFIELD

A bulldozer gives the *coup de grâce* to the William IV, after over 120 years of use. The destruction of Coburg Street opened up views of the medieval city wall, against which the houses had been built). The chocolate factory, by now owned by Nestlé, closed in 1996, as manufacturing has given way to retailing. It has been replaced by the new Chapelfield shopping centre. As with the older Castle Mall shopping centre, there is a great deal of history behind – and underneath – the contemporary façades.

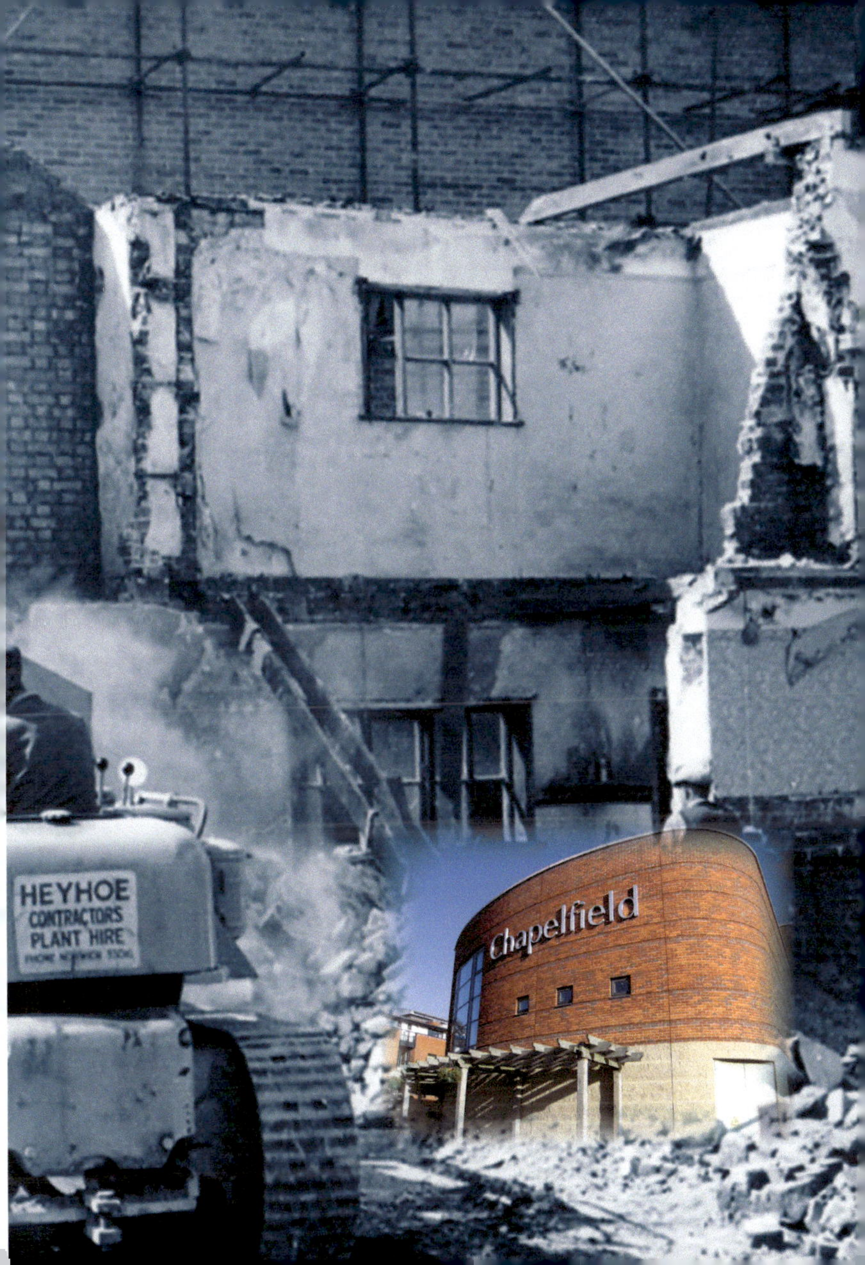
HEYHOE
CONTRACTORS
PLANT HIRE
Chapelfield

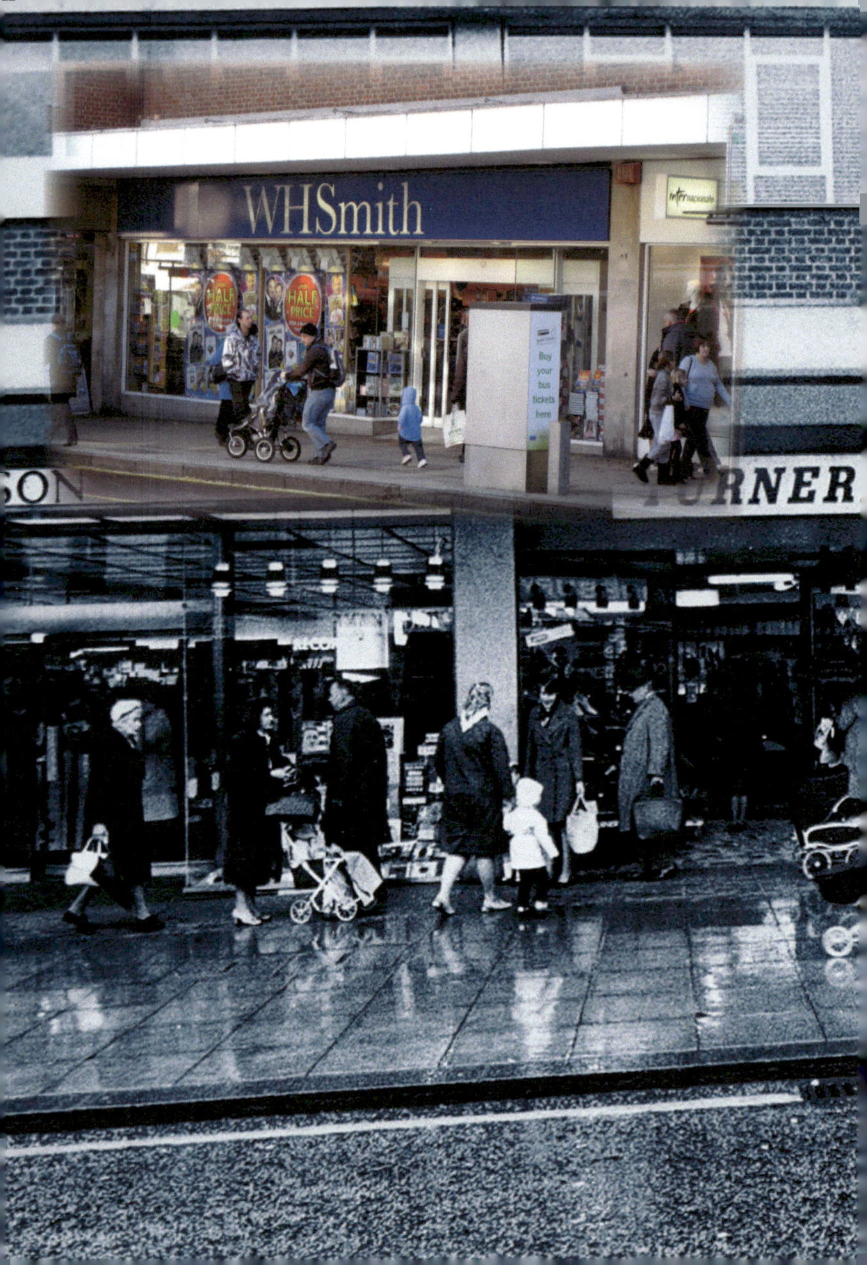

WHSmith
internazionale
HALF PRICE
HALF PRICE
Buy
your
bus
tickets
here
SON
TURNER

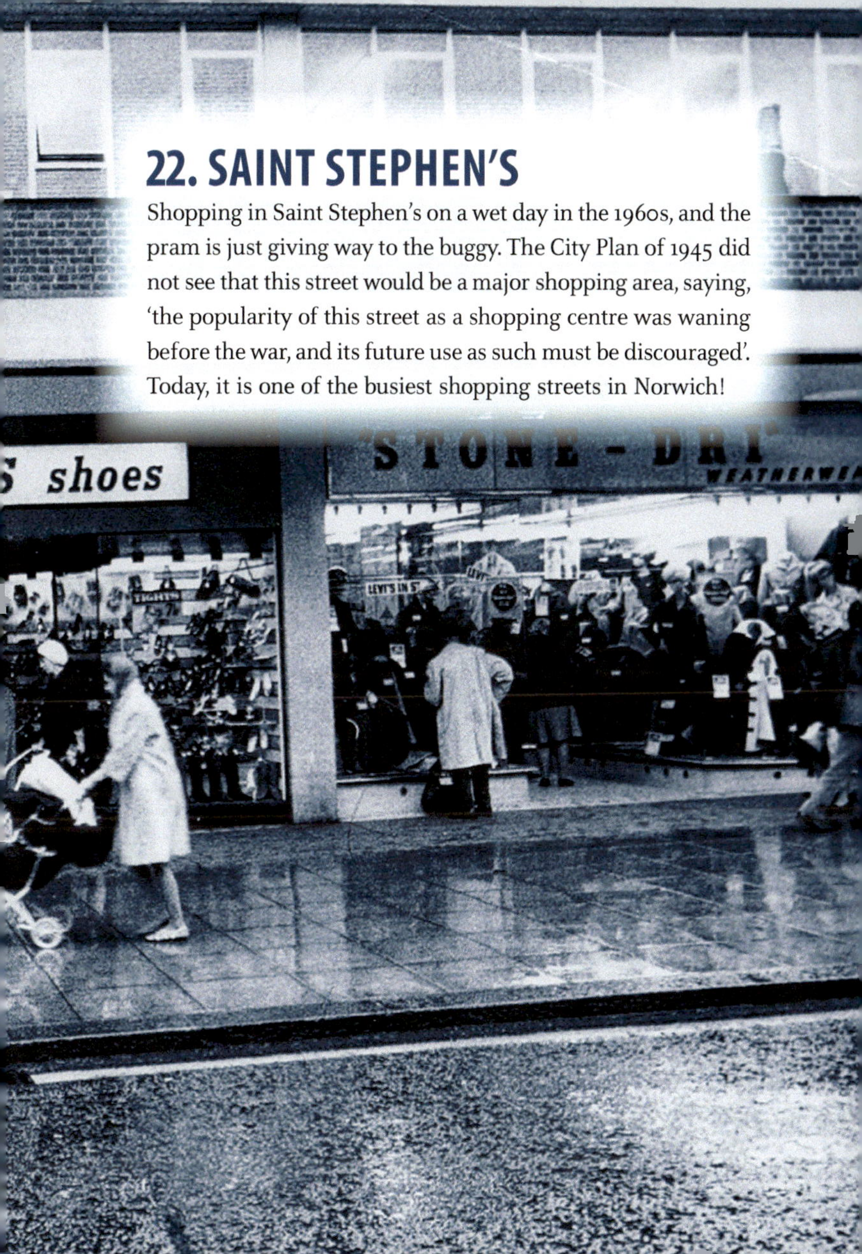

22. SAINT STEPHEN'S

Shopping in Saint Stephen's on a wet day in the 1960s, and the pram is just giving way to the buggy. The City Plan of 1945 did not see that this street would be a major shopping area, saying, 'the popularity of this street as a shopping centre was waning before the war, and its future use as such must be discouraged'. Today, it is one of the busiest shopping streets in Norwich!

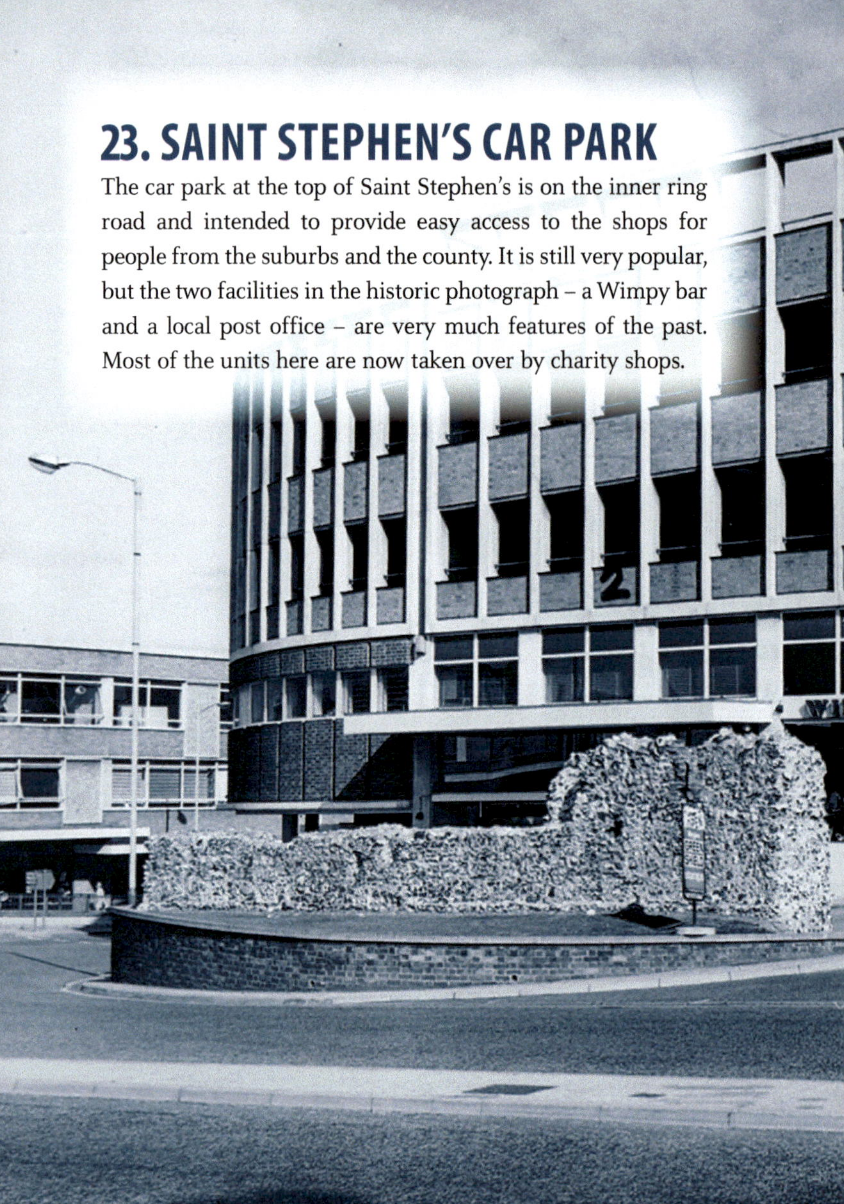

23. SAINT STEPHEN'S CAR PARK

The car park at the top of Saint Stephen's is on the inner ring road and intended to provide easy access to the shops for people from the suburbs and the county. It is still very popular, but the two facilities in the historic photograph – a Wimpy bar and a local post office – are very much features of the past. Most of the units here are now taken over by charity shops.

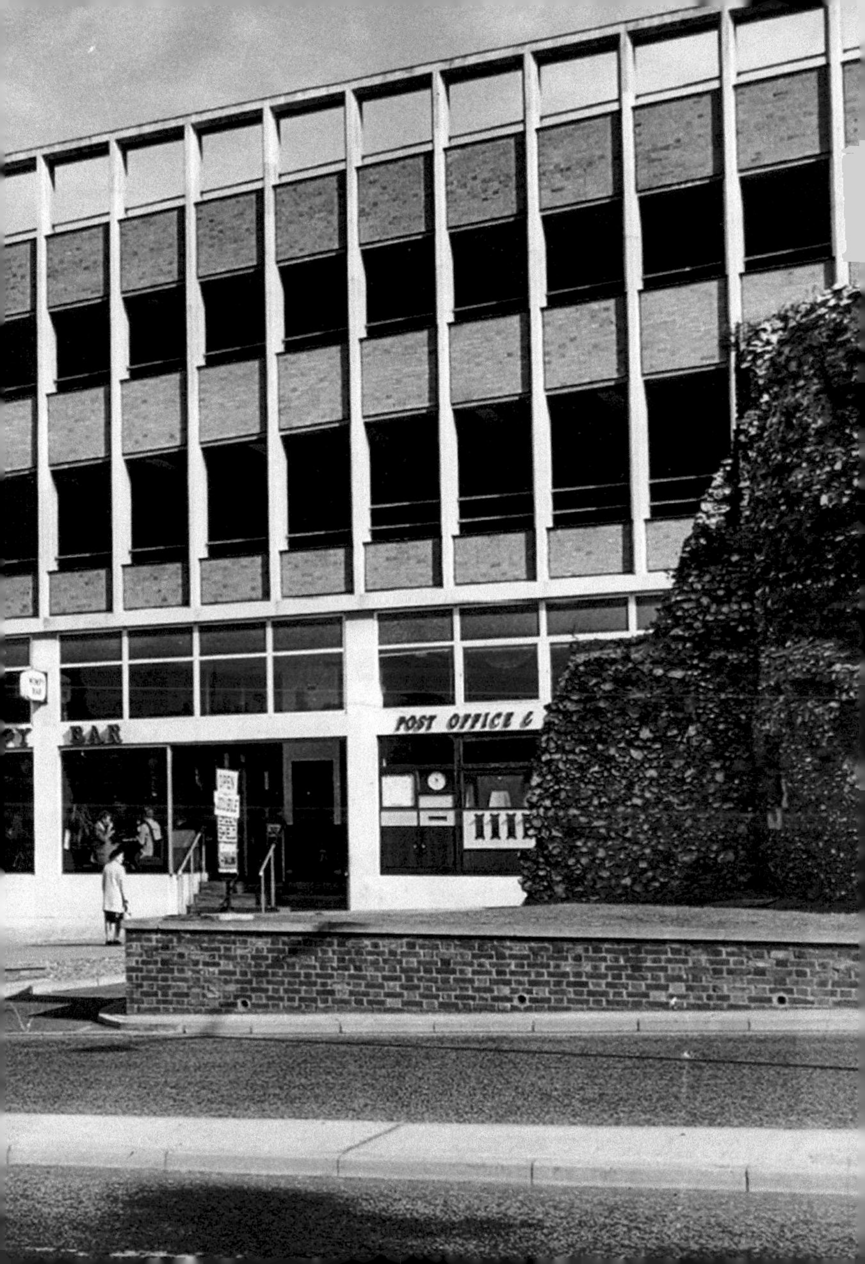
POST OFFICE
BAR

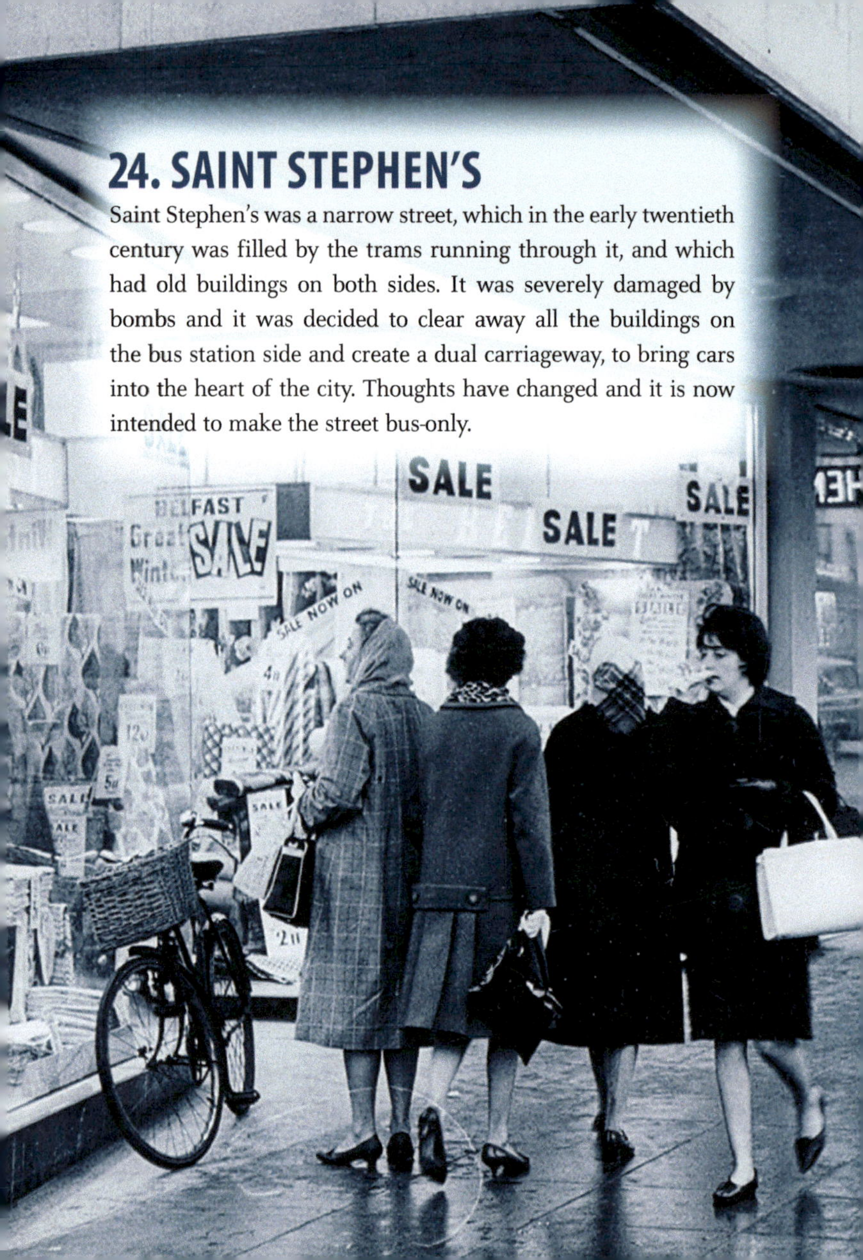

24. SAINT STEPHEN'S

Saint Stephen's was a narrow street, which in the early twentieth century was filled by the trams running through it, and which had old buildings on both sides. It was severely damaged by bombs and it was decided to clear away all the buildings on the bus station side and create a dual carriageway, to bring cars into the heart of the city. Thoughts have changed and it is now intended to make the street bus-only.

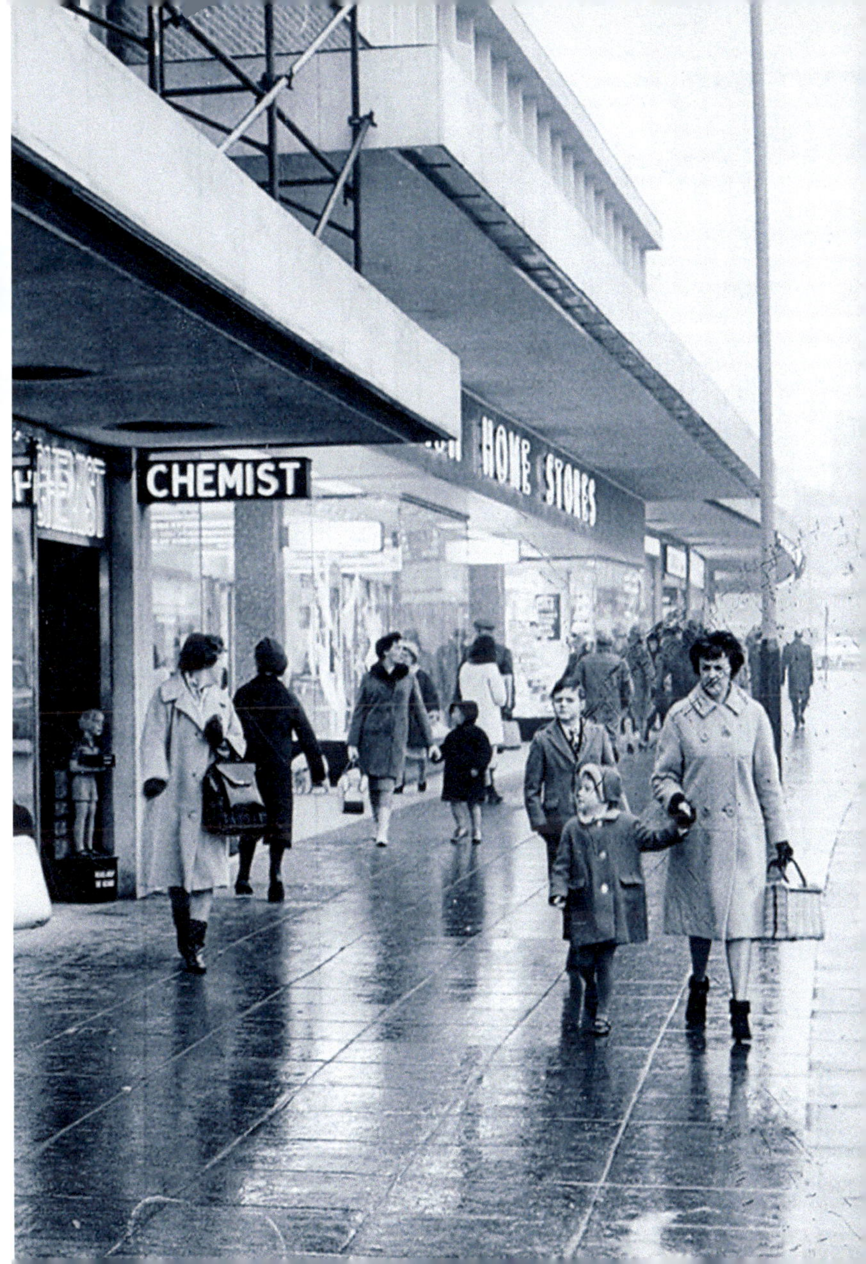

CHEMIST
HOME STORES

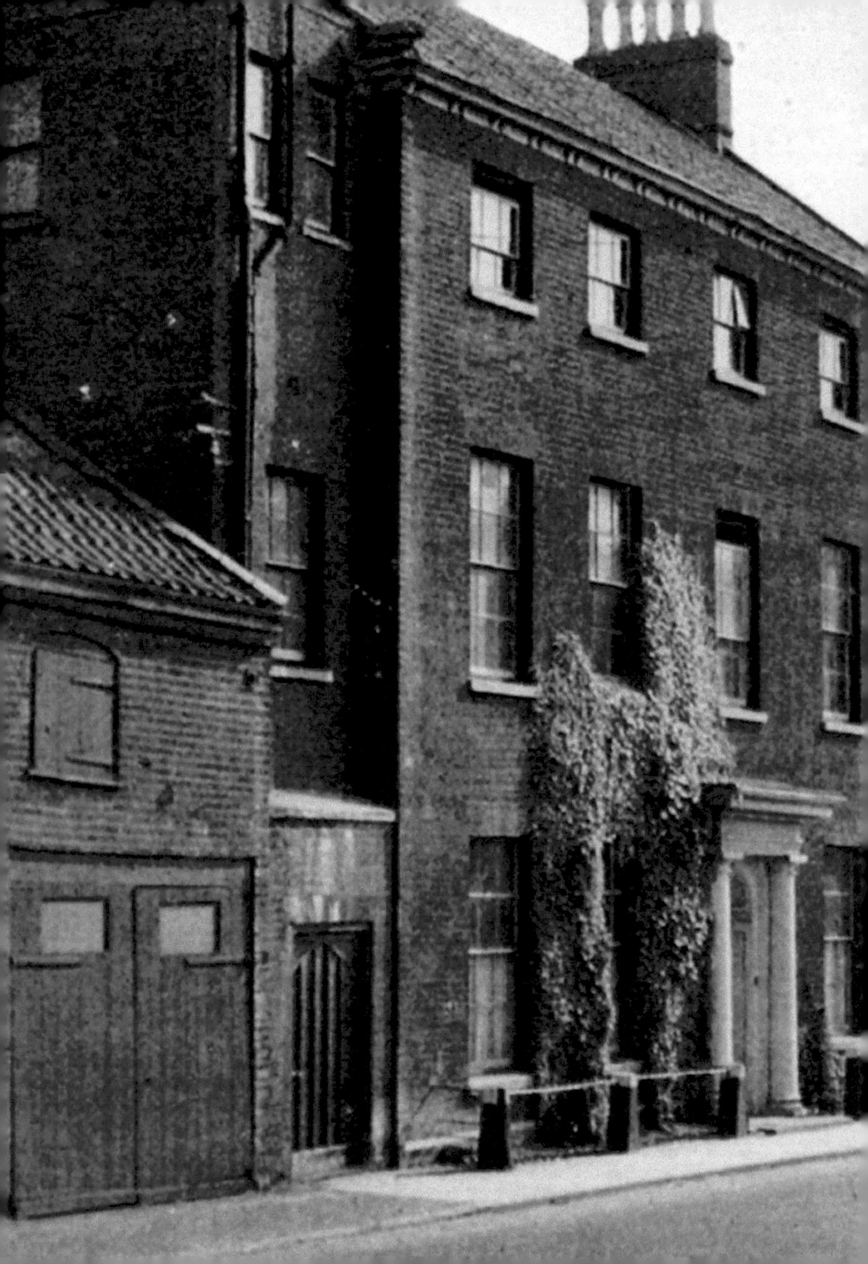

25. ALL SAINTS' GREEN

This street retains some of Norwich's best Georgian houses. William Darby, an early black resident of Norwich, was a butler in a house in this parish. His son, also William, went on to become the first black circus proprietor in Britain under the name of Pablo Fanque, and he is mentioned in a song on the Beatles' *Sergeant Pepper* album – probably the only inhabitant of Norwich to be so honoured.

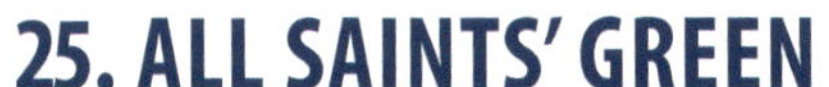

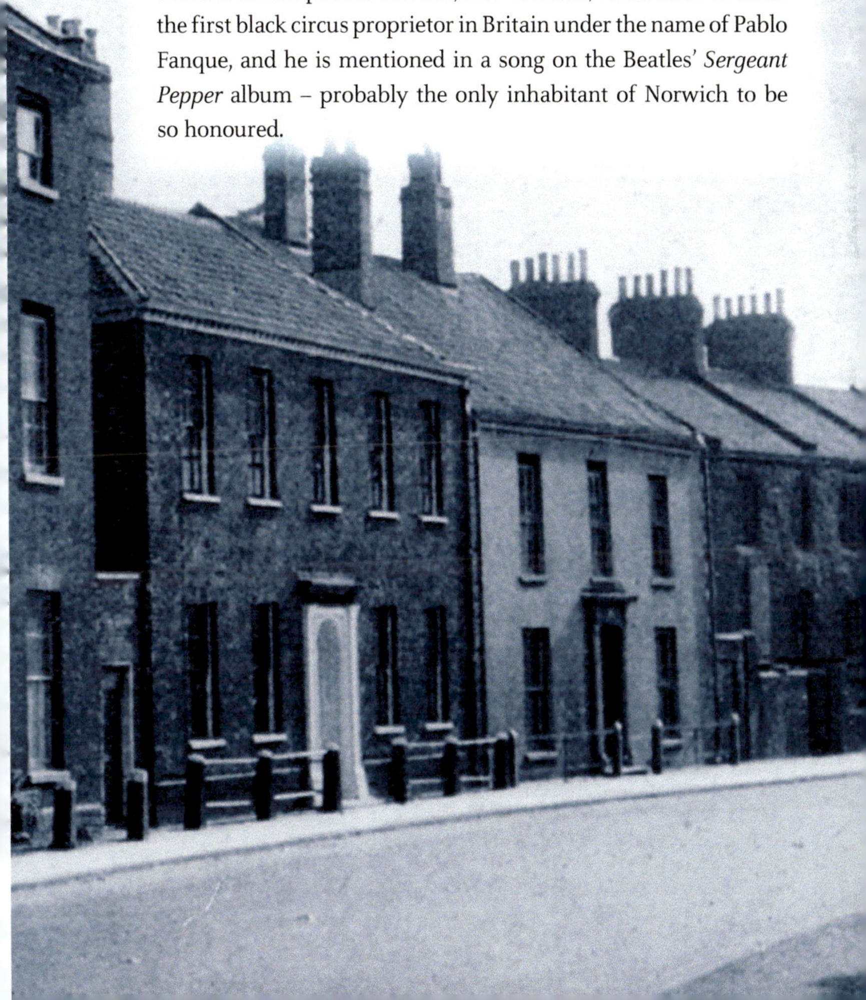

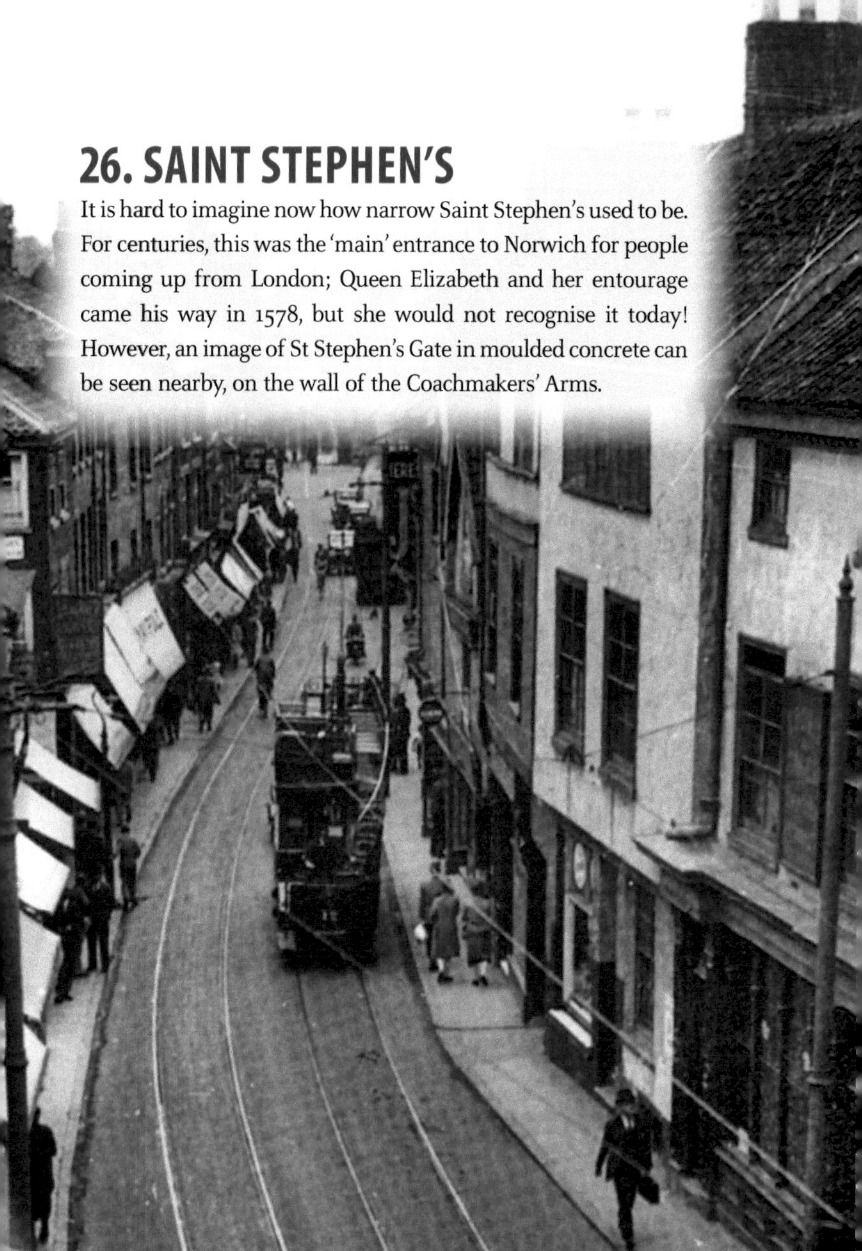

26. SAINT STEPHEN'S

It is hard to imagine now how narrow Saint Stephen's used to be. For centuries, this was the 'main' entrance to Norwich for people coming up from London; Queen Elizabeth and her entourage came his way in 1578, but she would not recognise it today! However, an image of St Stephen's Gate in moulded concrete can be seen nearby, on the wall of the Coachmakers' Arms.

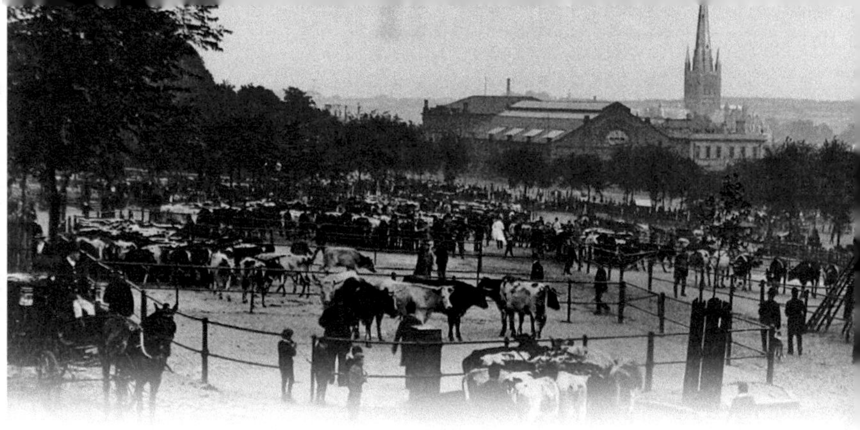

27. THE GOLDEN BALL

The historic photograph was taken from the upper window of the Golden Ball public house, now replaced by the offices of Eastern Counties Newspapers, and the statue in front of their building is indeed representative of the earlier name. In the distance is the back of one of Norwich's finest Victorian buildings, the Agricultural Hall, built in 1882 by J. B. Pearce.

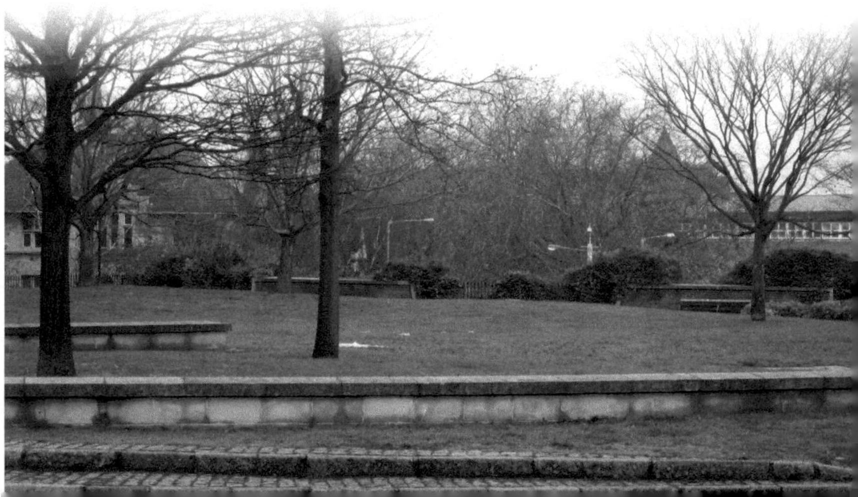

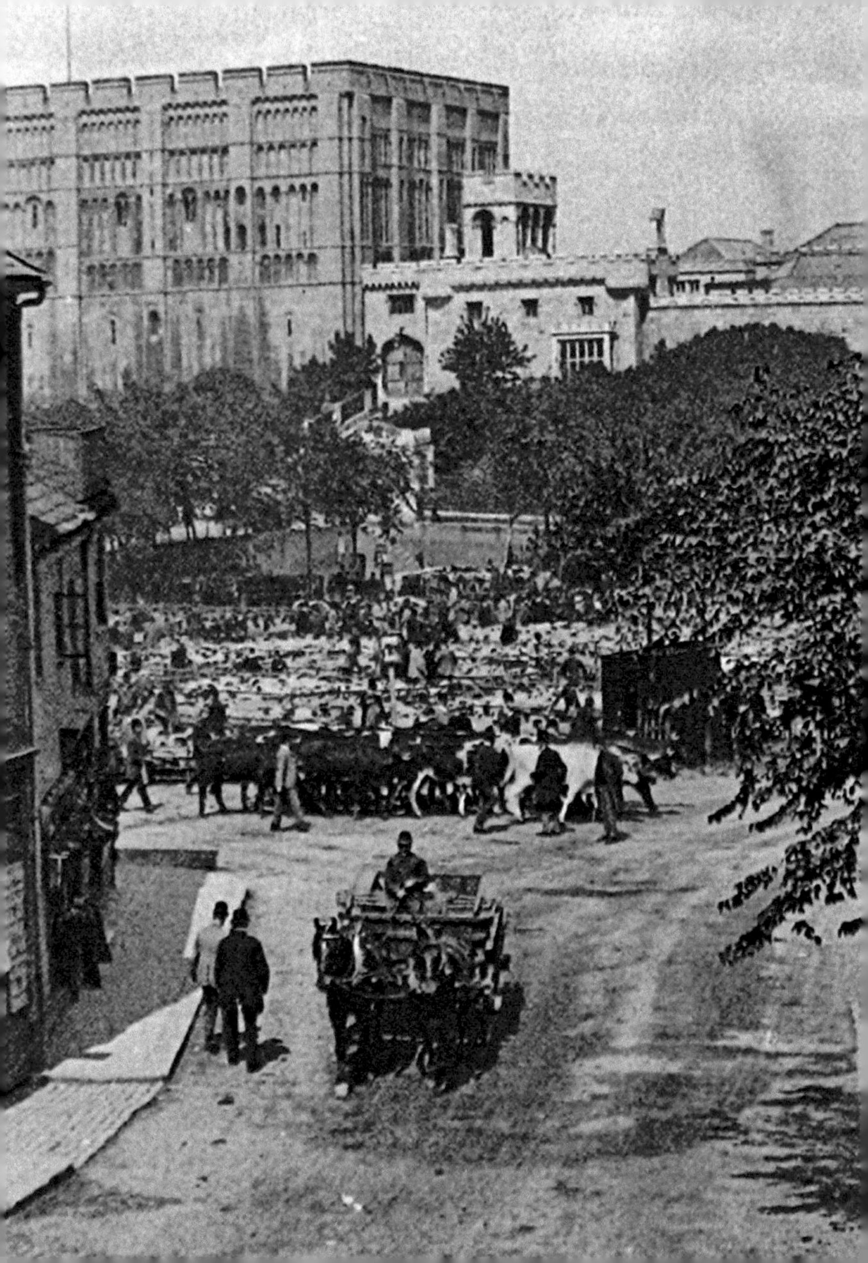

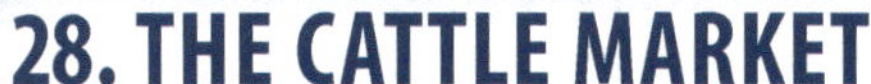

28. THE CATTLE MARKET

The two markets of Norwich stood for centuries on either side of the castle, like two lungs breathing life into the city. The cattle market literally brought life into the heart of Norwich: cows, sheep, pigs and poultry were brought here along all the main roads into the city. Like any good market, it was surrounded by public houses, some of which still flourish despite the disappearance of the market traders.

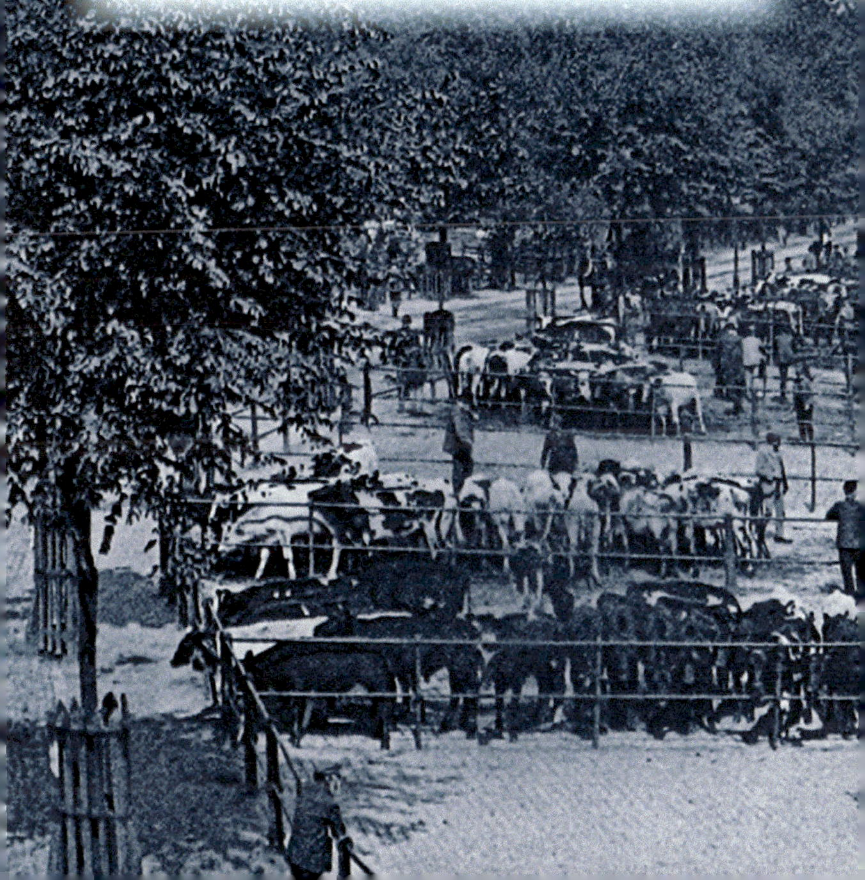

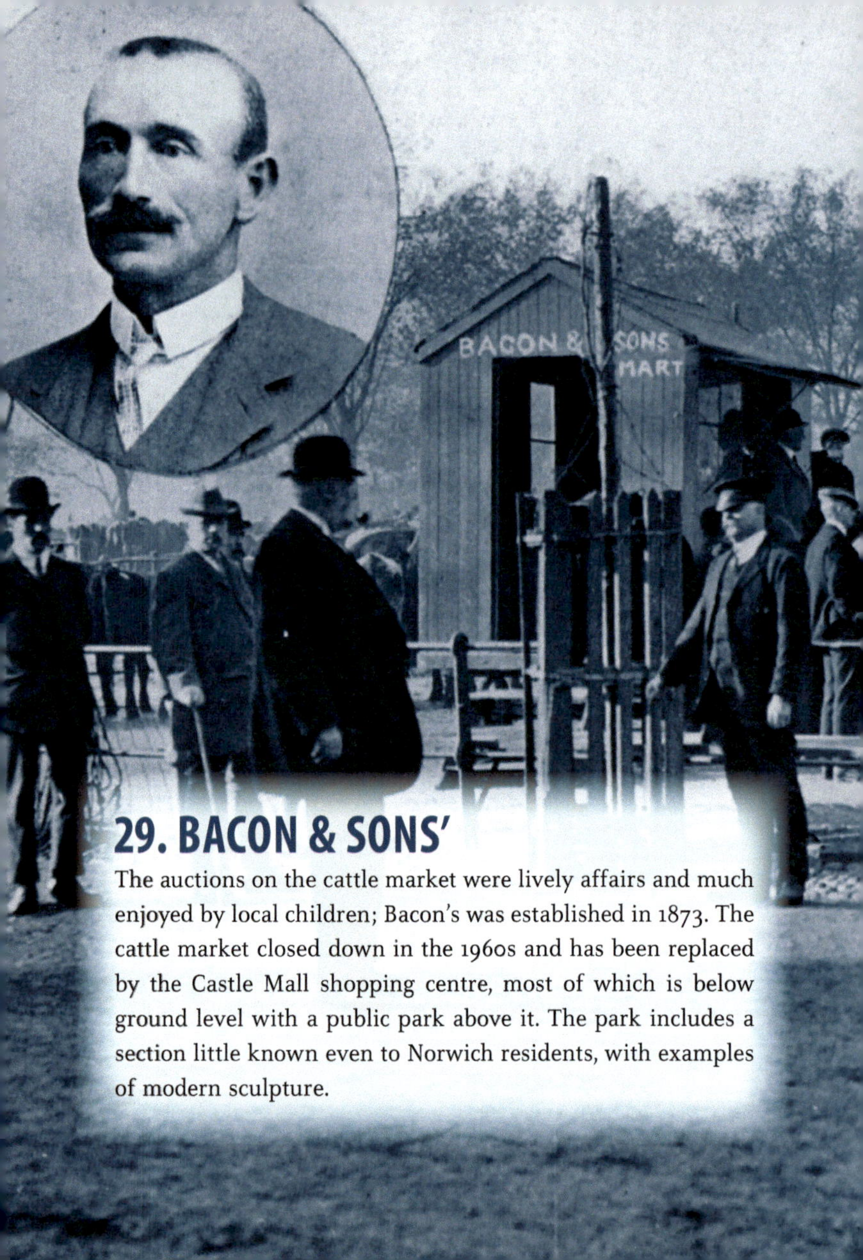

29. BACON & SONS'

The auctions on the cattle market were lively affairs and much enjoyed by local children; Bacon's was established in 1873. The cattle market closed down in the 1960s and has been replaced by the Castle Mall shopping centre, most of which is below ground level with a public park above it. The park includes a section little known even to Norwich residents, with examples of modern sculpture.

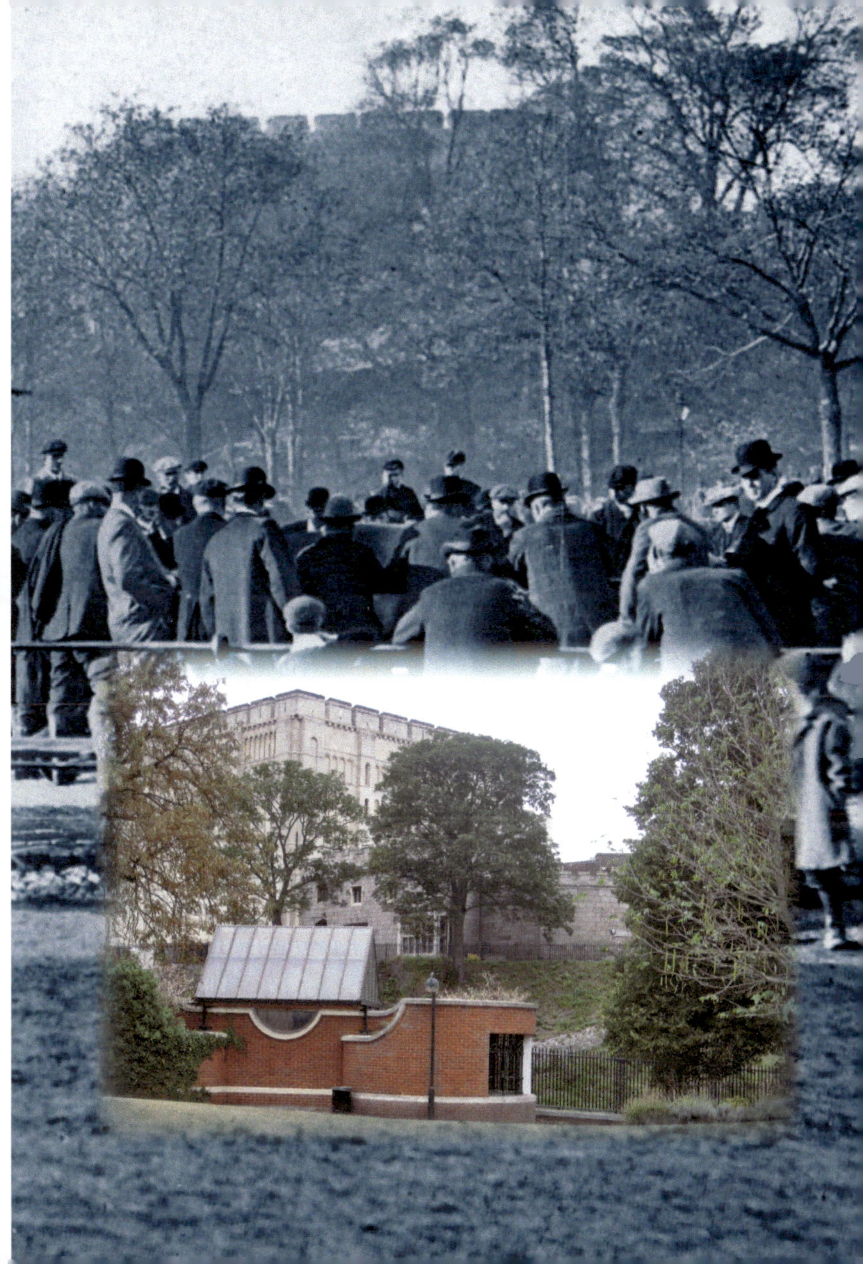

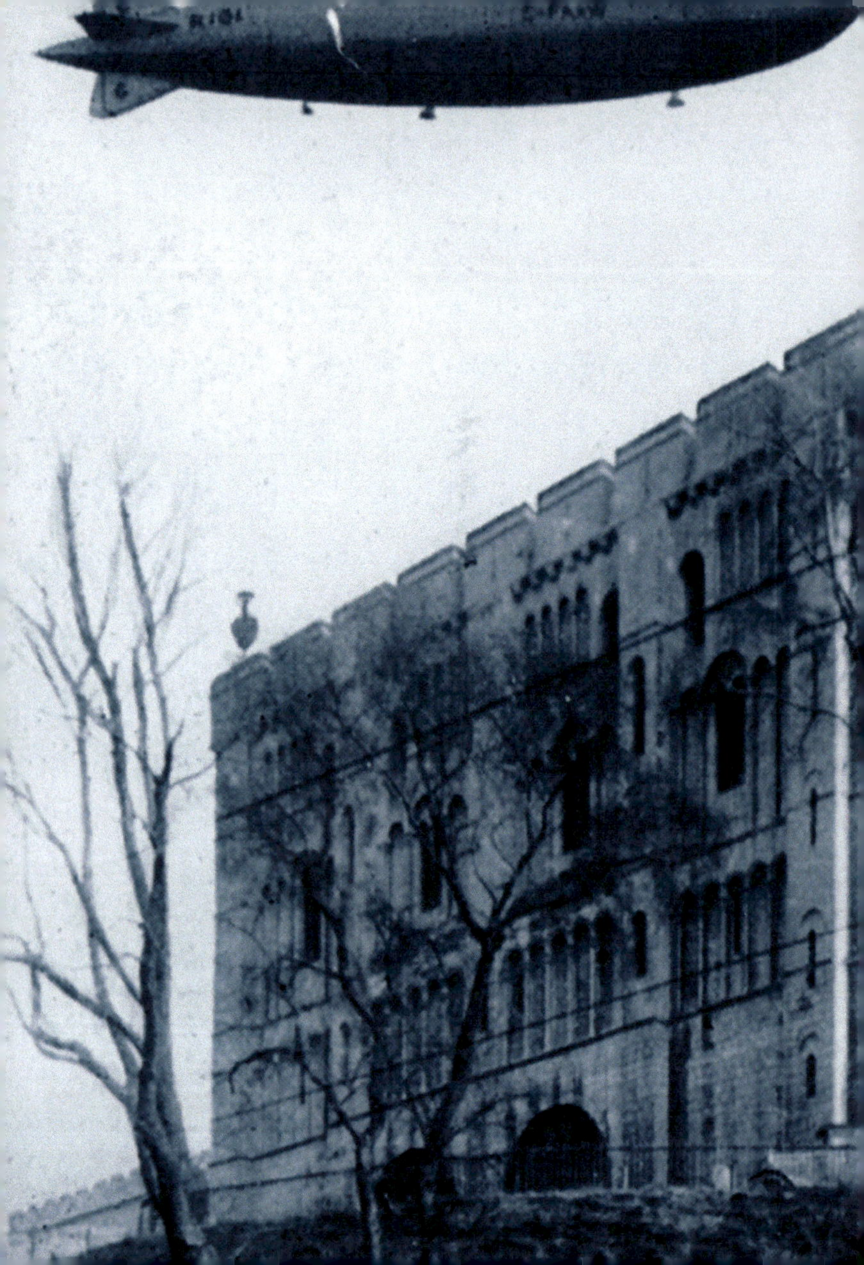

30. NORWICH CASTLE

The historic photograph captures the airship R101 as she flies over Norwich on 1 November 1929. She had taken off from Pulham; the airship base there is now seen on the village sign. The urn-like object on the castle is the Norwich Time Ball. This relates to a time when clocks and watches were not so reliable as today: the ball would fall with a loud crash at an exact time every day, so that people could adjust their watches.

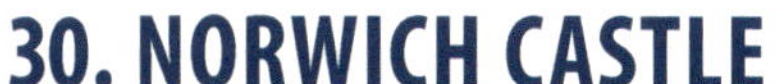

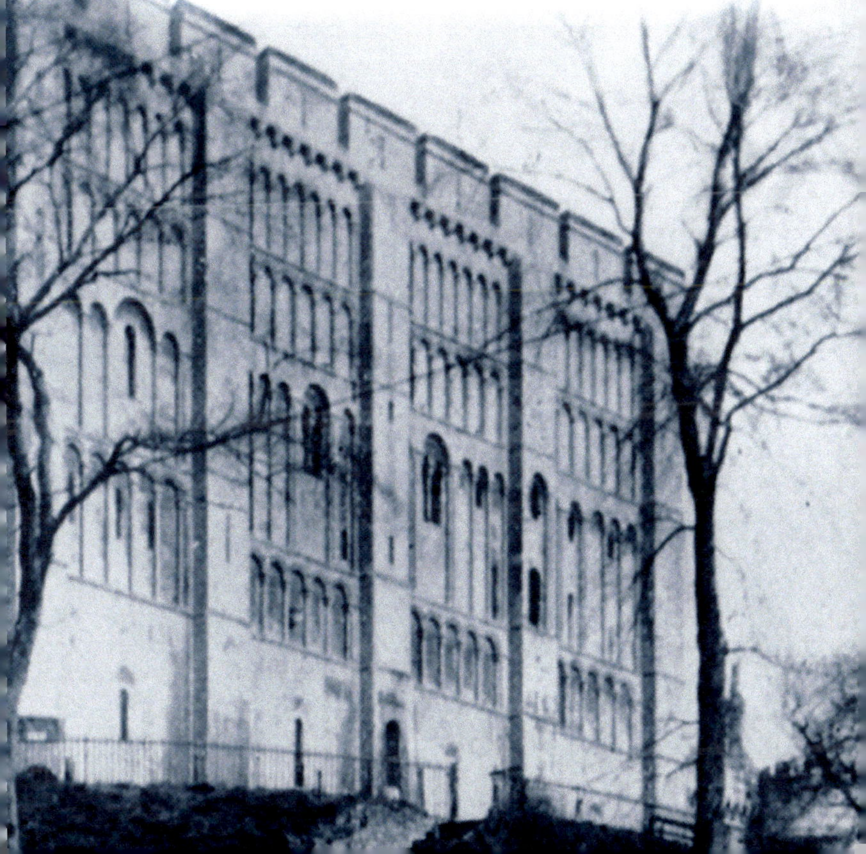

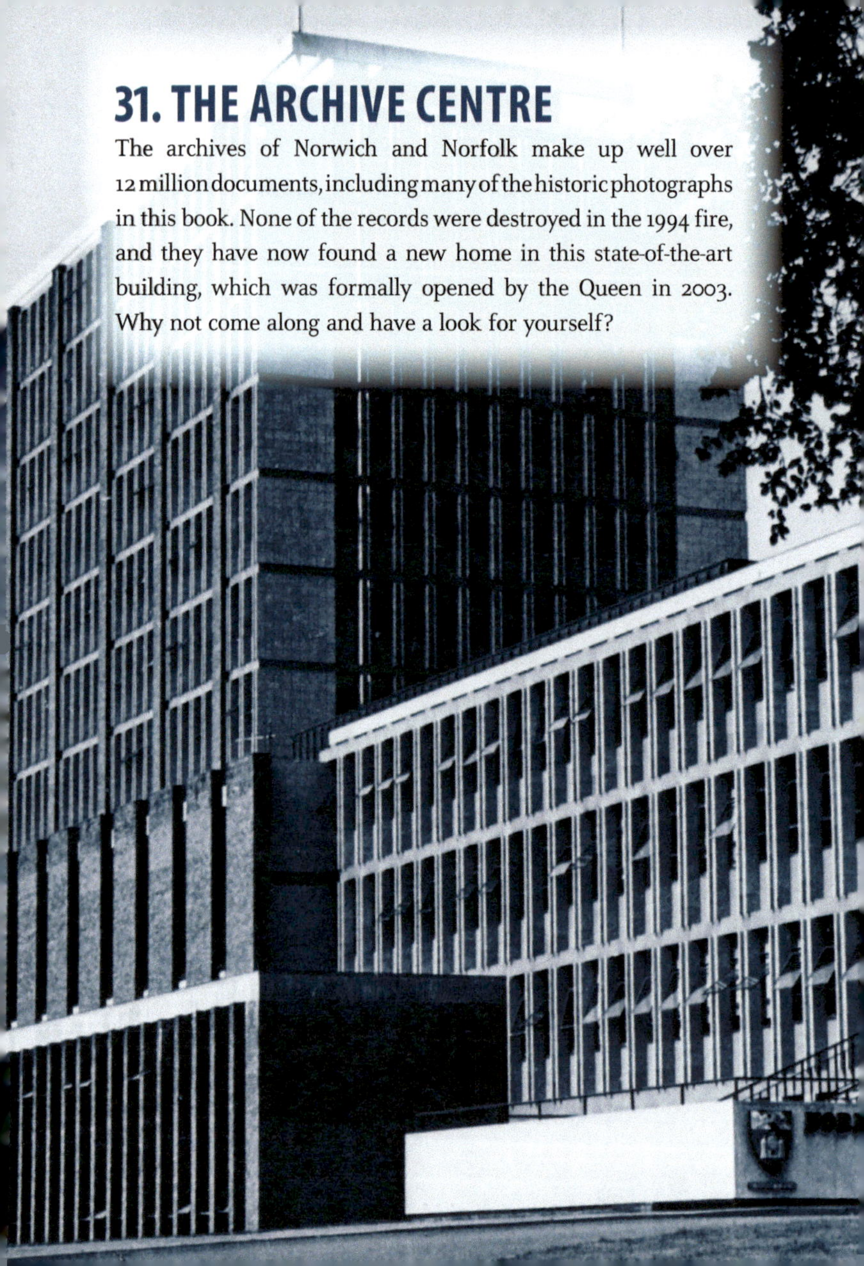

31. THE ARCHIVE CENTRE

The archives of Norwich and Norfolk make up well over 12 million documents, including many of the historic photographs in this book. None of the records were destroyed in the 1994 fire, and they have now found a new home in this state-of-the-art building, which was formally opened by the Queen in 2003. Why not come along and have a look for yourself?

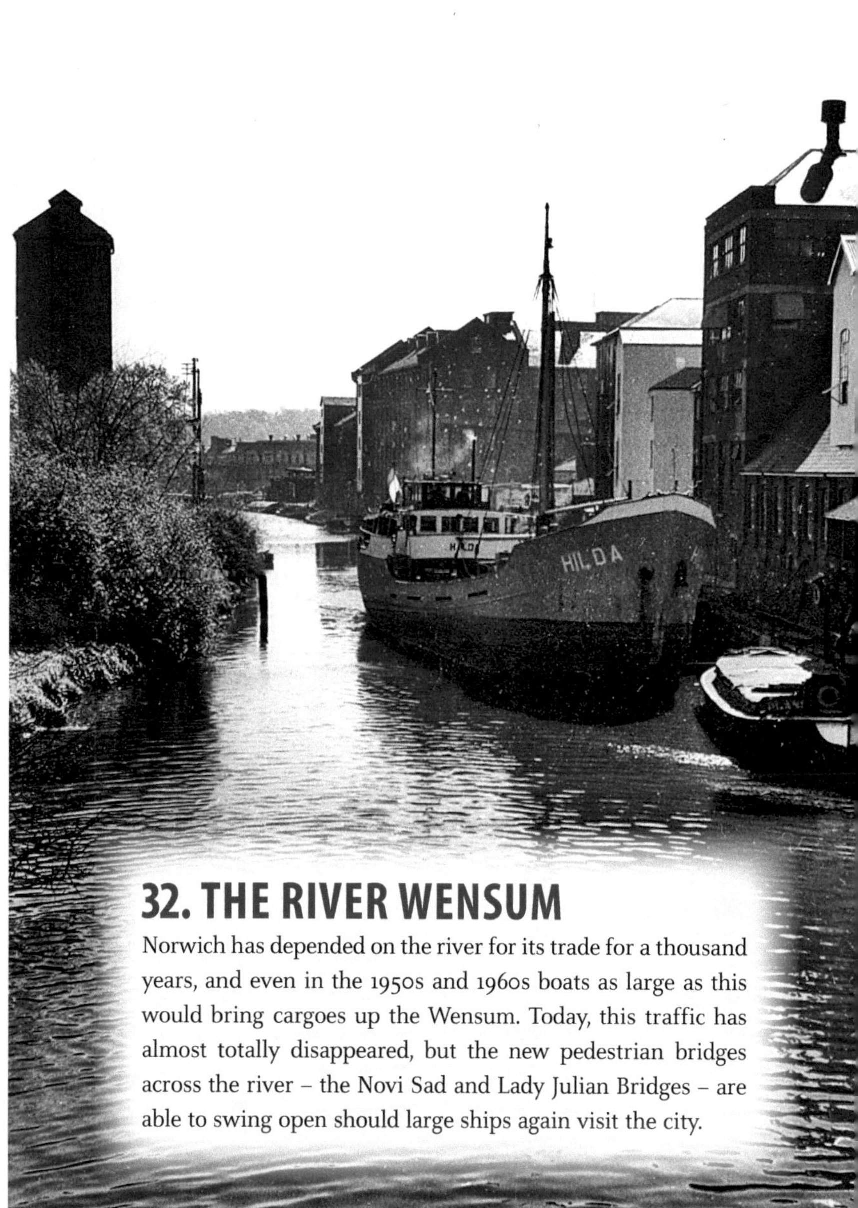

32. THE RIVER WENSUM

Norwich has depended on the river for its trade for a thousand years, and even in the 1950s and 1960s boats as large as this would bring cargoes up the Wensum. Today, this traffic has almost totally disappeared, but the new pedestrian bridges across the river – the Novi Sad and Lady Julian Bridges – are able to swing open should large ships again visit the city.

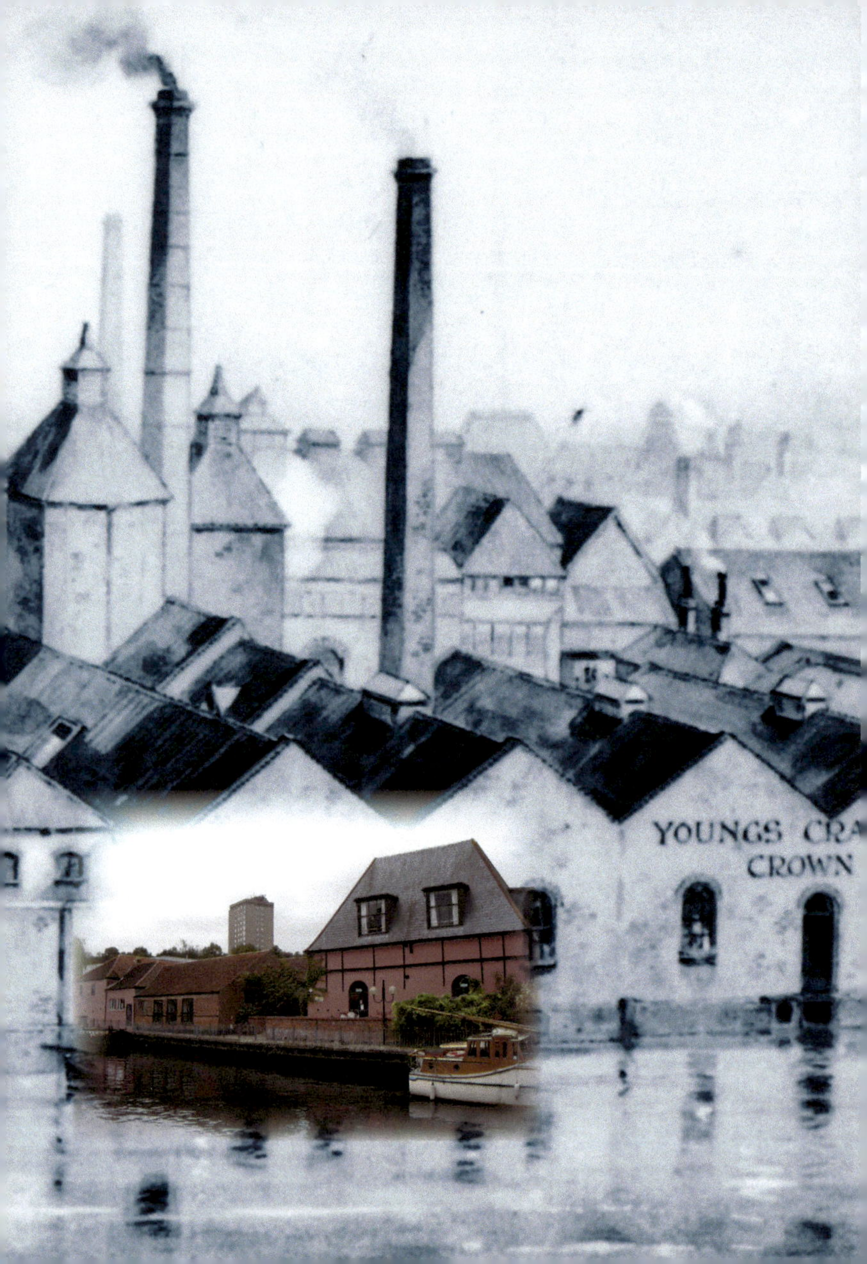
YOUNGS CRA
CROWN

33. THE CROWN BREWERY

There were four large breweries in Norwich in the nineteenth century and the river was a key element in their existence for the carriage of malt and barley. The Crown Brewery has given way to Wensum Lodge, a centre for adult education, while one of the maltings has been successfully converted into apartments. The entrance gates to Wensum Lodge still bear the emblem of the Crown Brewery on their gateposts.

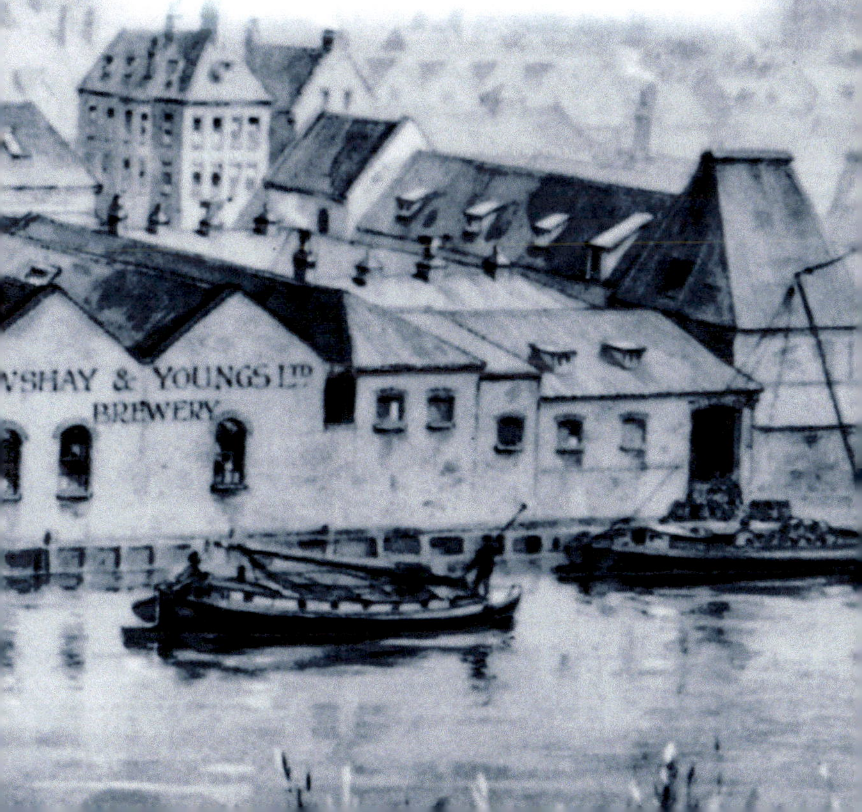

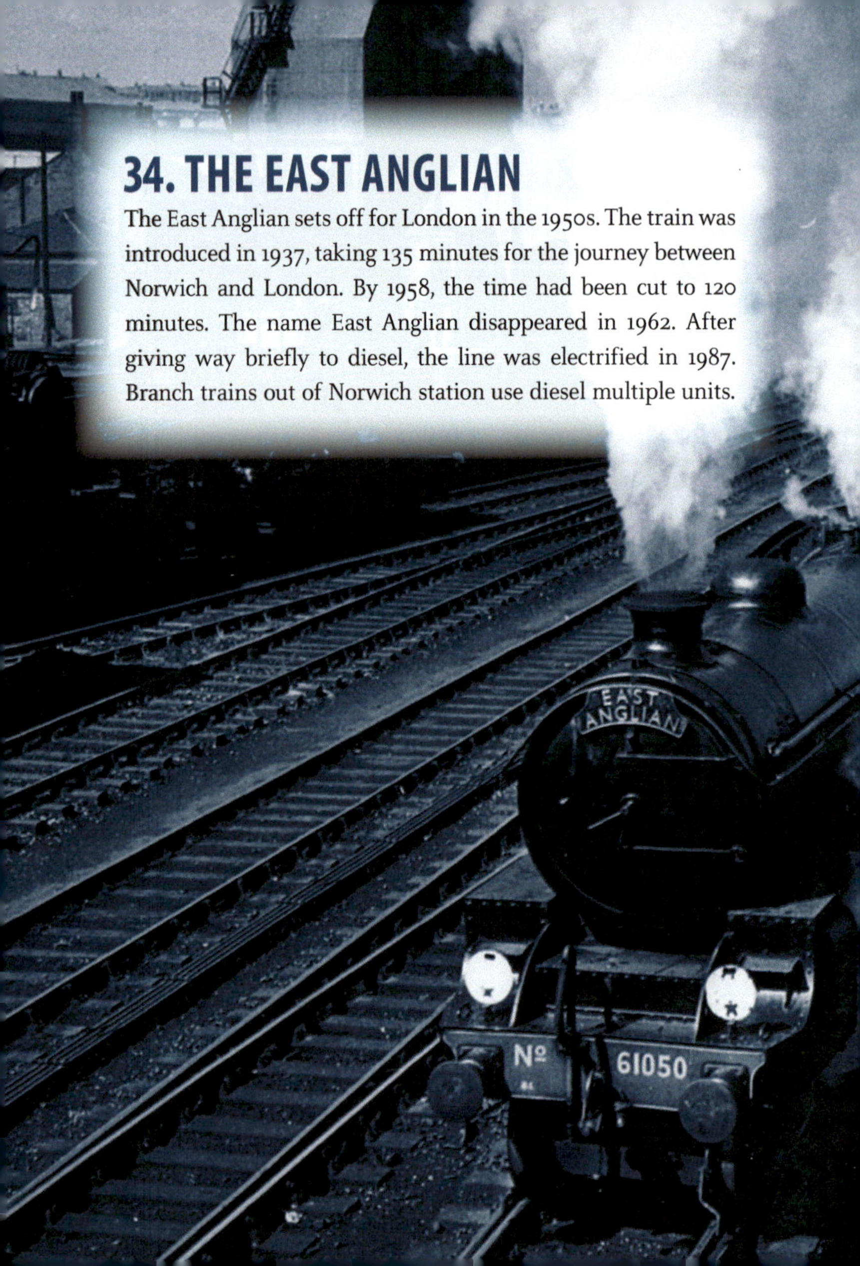

34. THE EAST ANGLIAN

The East Anglian sets off for London in the 1950s. The train was introduced in 1937, taking 135 minutes for the journey between Norwich and London. By 1958, the time had been cut to 120 minutes. The name East Anglian disappeared in 1962. After giving way briefly to diesel, the line was electrified in 1987. Branch trains out of Norwich station use diesel multiple units.

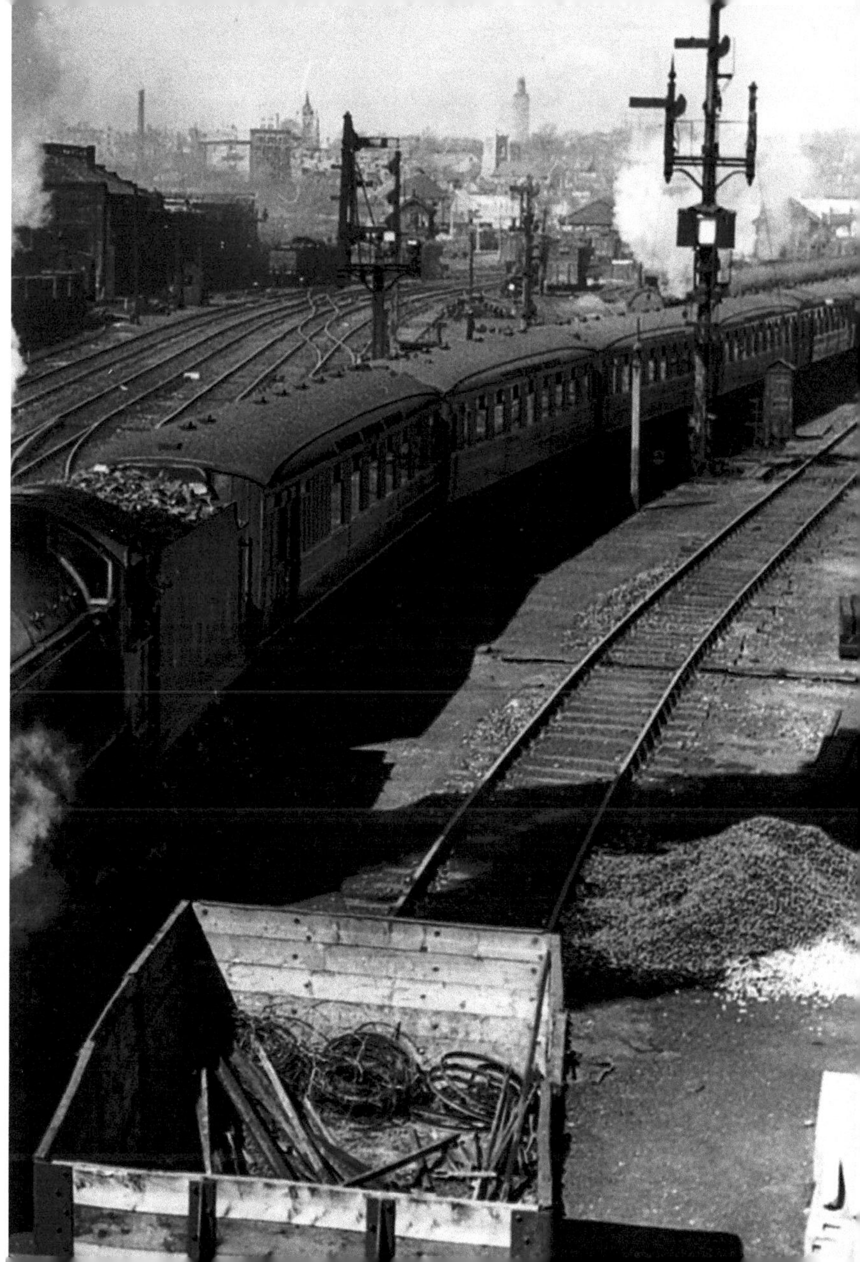

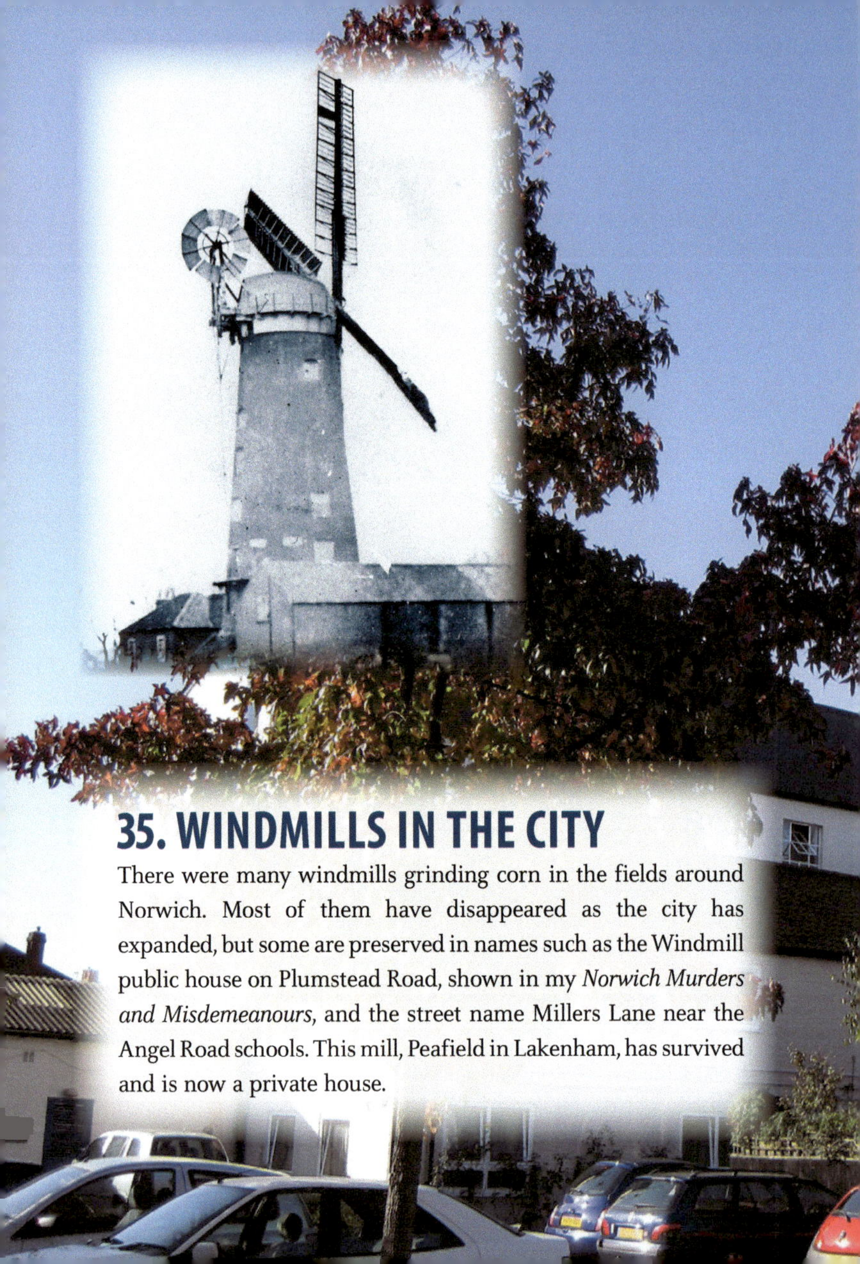

35. WINDMILLS IN THE CITY

There were many windmills grinding corn in the fields around Norwich. Most of them have disappeared as the city has expanded, but some are preserved in names such as the Windmill public house on Plumstead Road, shown in my *Norwich Murders and Misdemeanours*, and the street name Millers Lane near the Angel Road schools. This mill, Peafield in Lakenham, has survived and is now a private house.

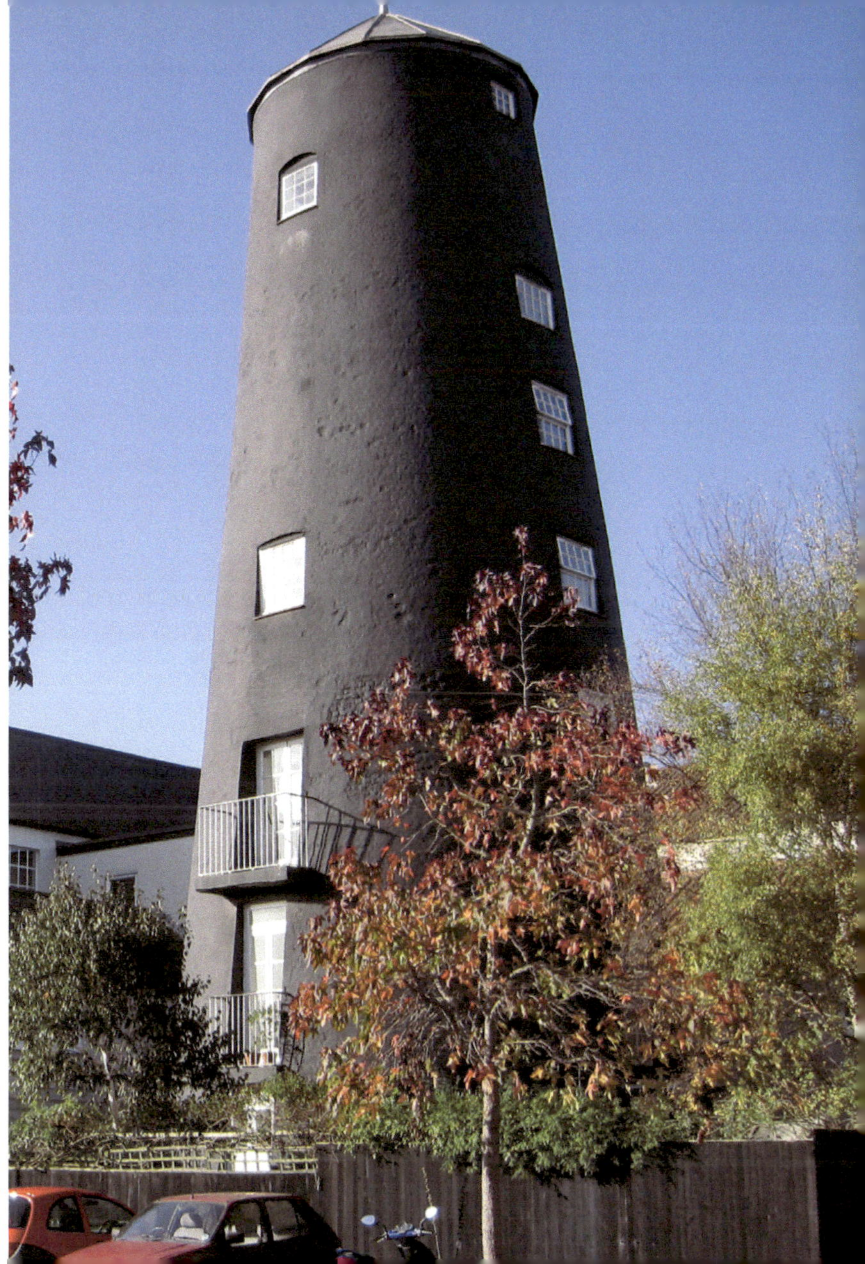

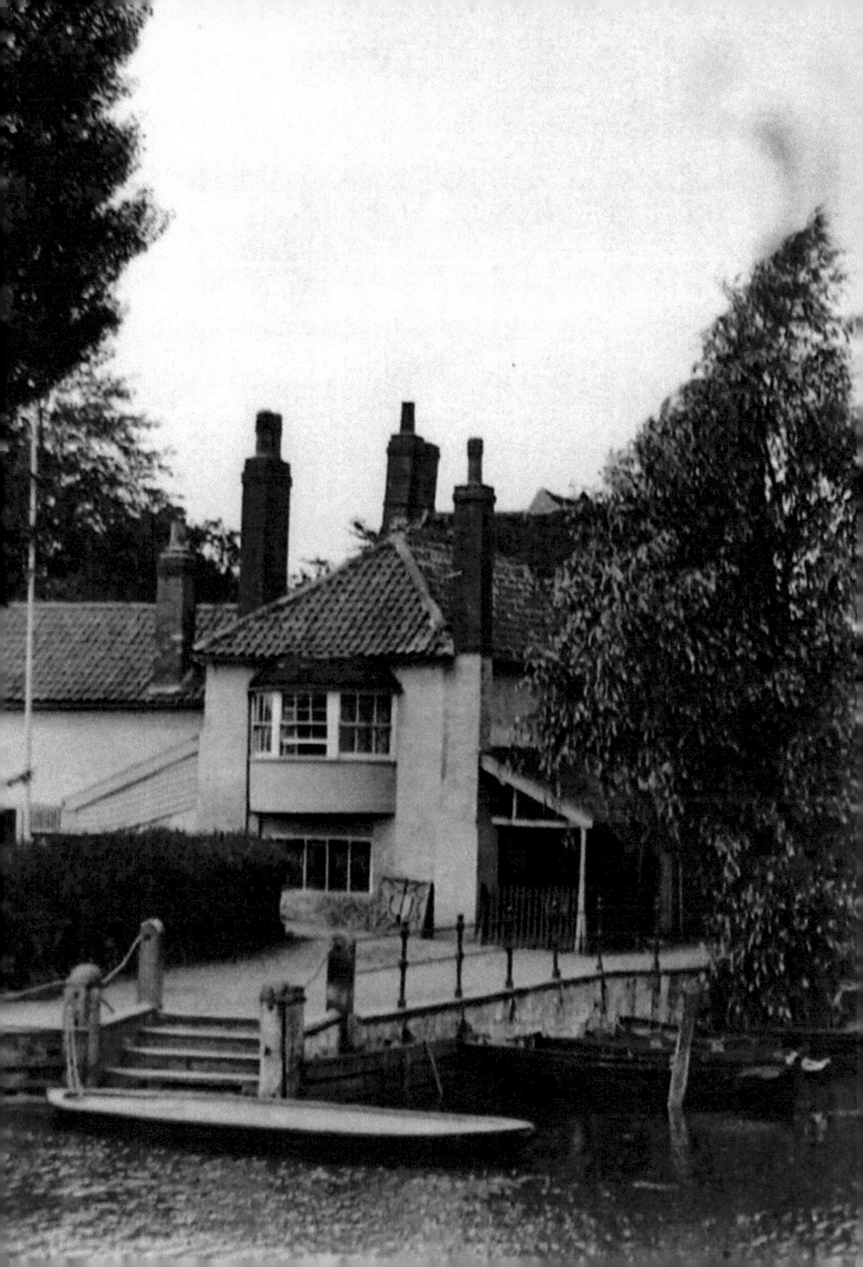

36. PULL'S FERRY

Further downstream, Pull's Ferry is one of the most painted and photographed spots in the city. There was originally a canal running underneath the arch; the stone of which the cathedral is built was transported all the way from Normandy by sea and river. Pull is actually the name of the ferryman in late Victorian times, as before his time the ferry was called Sandling's Ferry after the ferryman during the reign of the first Queen Elizabeth!

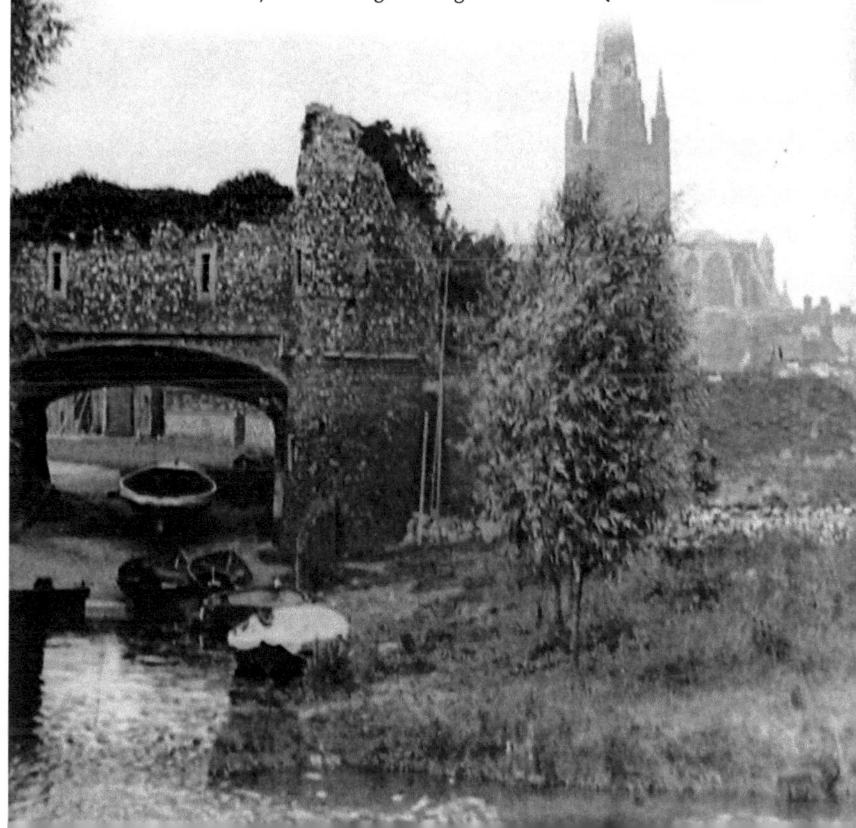

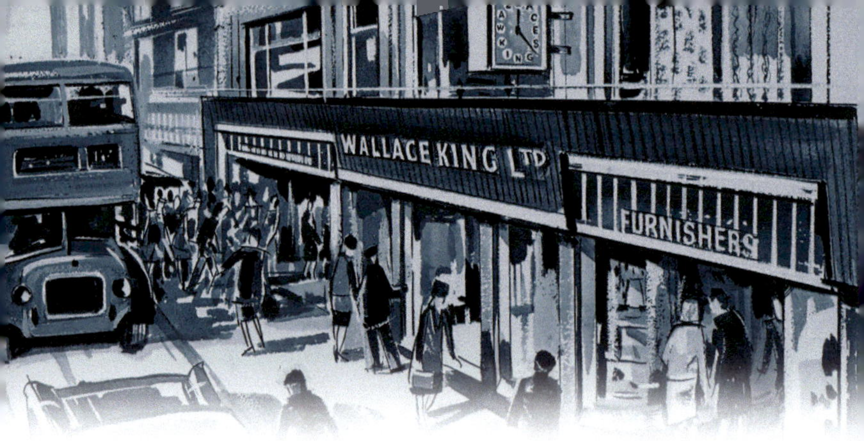

37. WALLACE KING

One of the iconic firms of the city was the furnishing store of Wallace King Ltd on the Prince of Wales Road. This building is one of the few in Norwich that can be described as art nouveau in style. Today, shops have given way to restaurants and nightclubs along the whole length of the street, which was originally built to connect the railway station to the centre of the city.

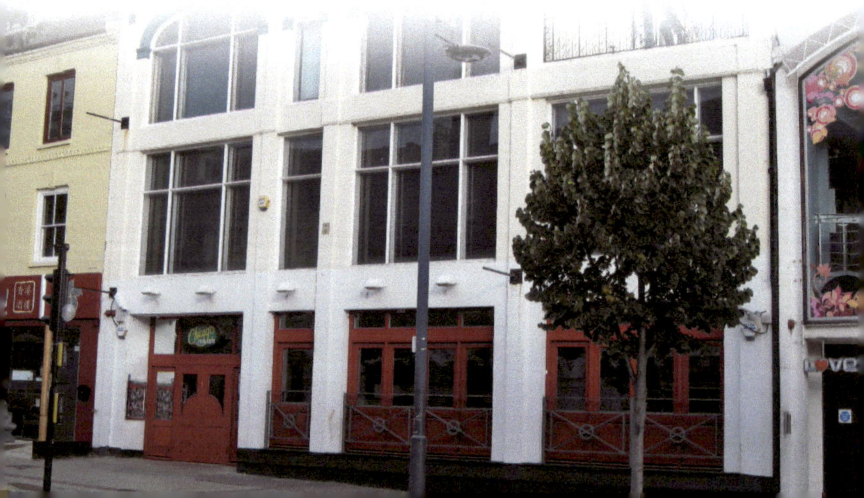

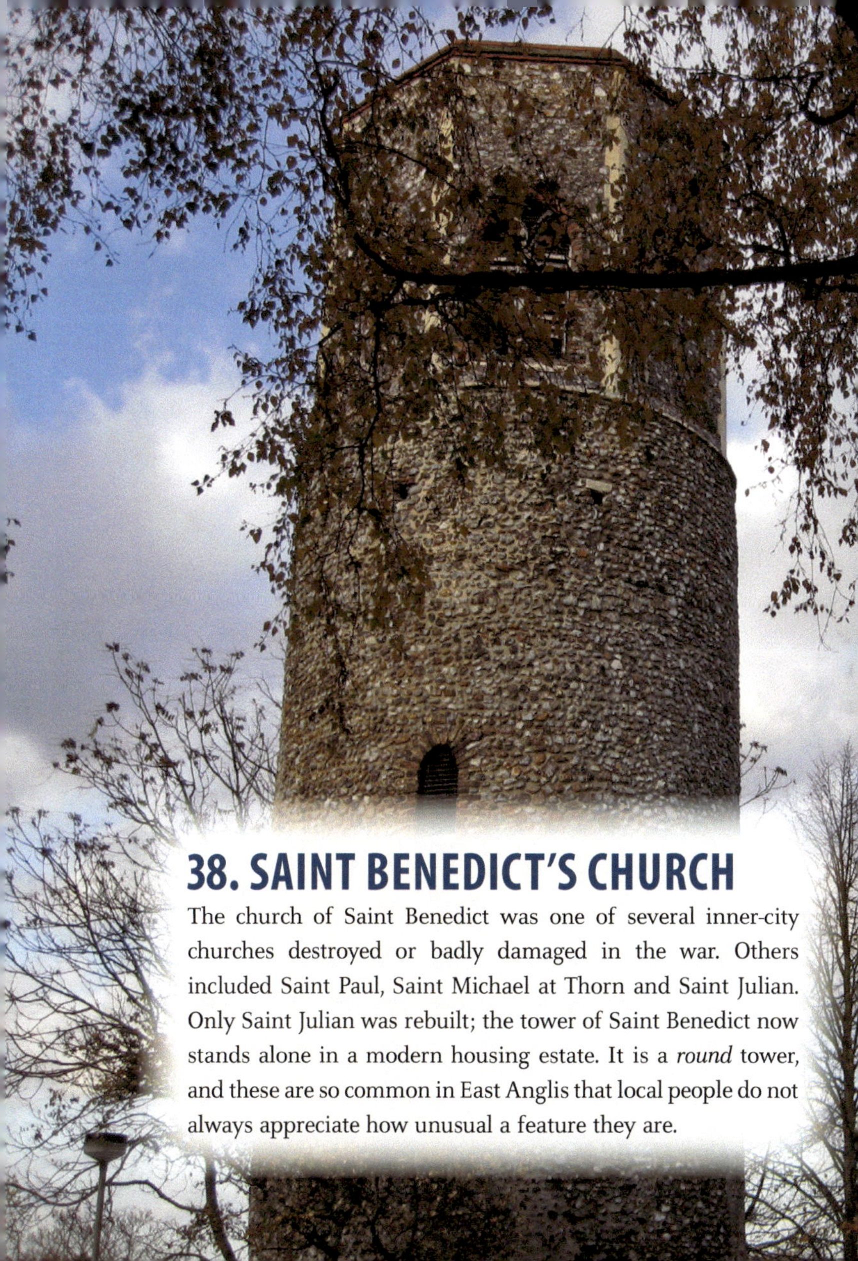

38. SAINT BENEDICT'S CHURCH

The church of Saint Benedict was one of several inner-city churches destroyed or badly damaged in the war. Others included Saint Paul, Saint Michael at Thorn and Saint Julian. Only Saint Julian was rebuilt; the tower of Saint Benedict now stands alone in a modern housing estate. It is a *round* tower, and these are so common in East Anglis that local people do not always appreciate how unusual a feature they are.

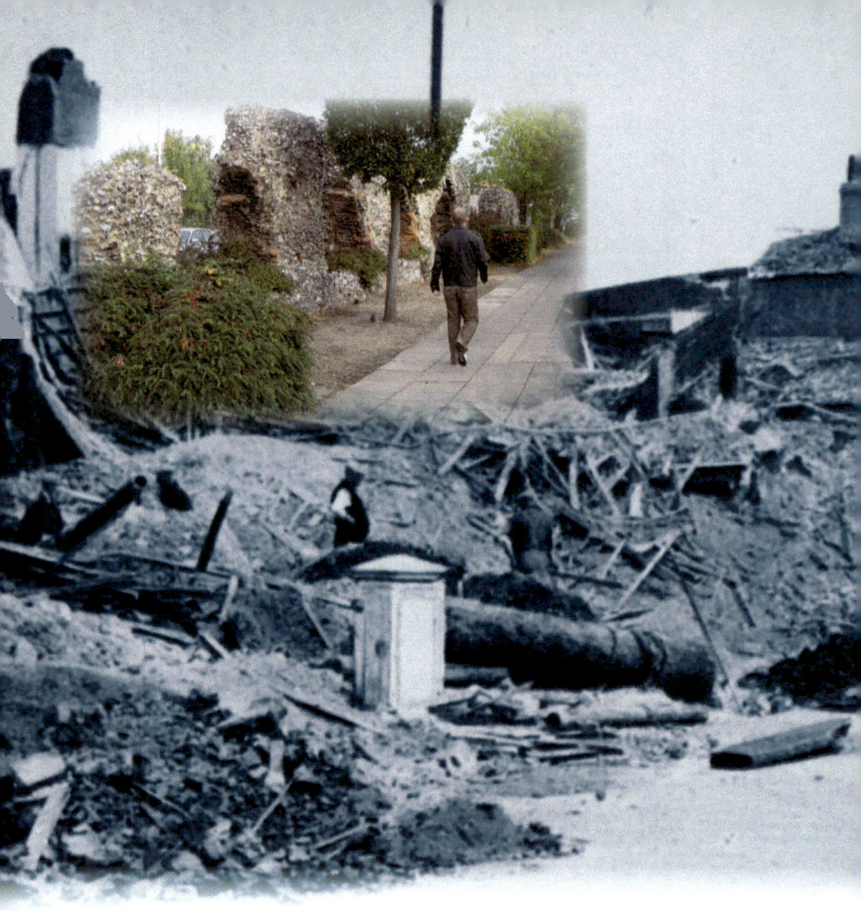

39. SAINT BENEDICT'S

The area where St Benedict's meets Grapes Hill was perhaps the part of
Norwich that was worst hit during the war, especially by the attacks on
27/28 and 29/30 April 1942. Norwich was one of the cities chosen by the

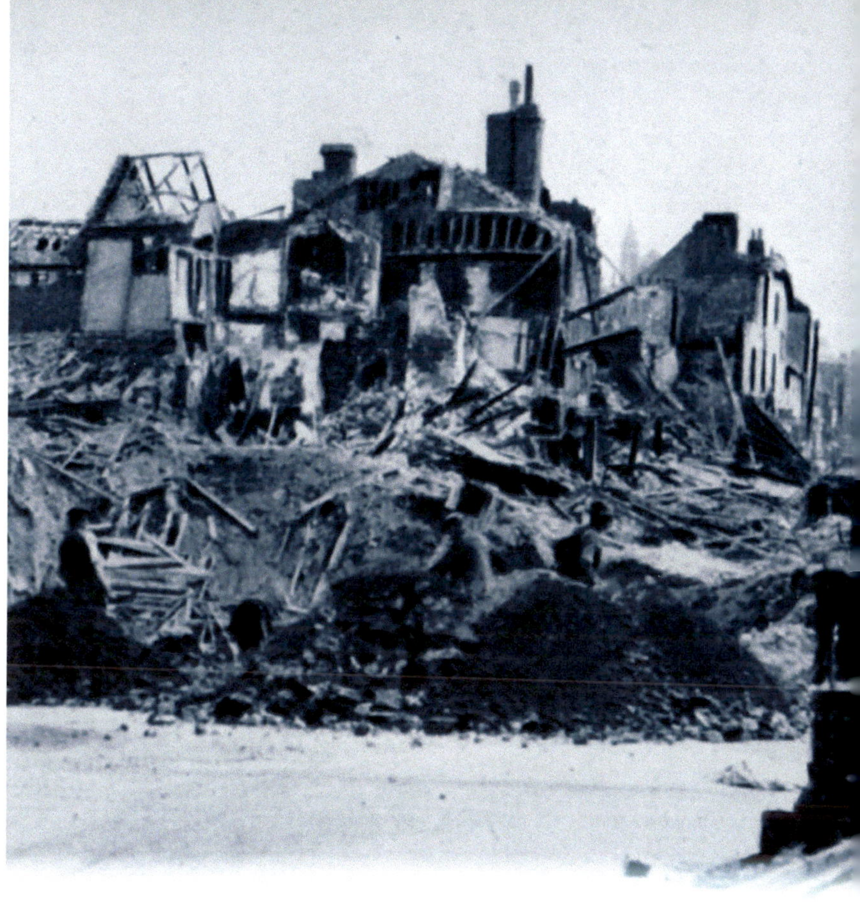

Germans because it was highly praised in Baedeker's guidebook, and for this reason these raids are often called the Baedeker raids. The devastation created an opportunity for large-scale reconstruction.

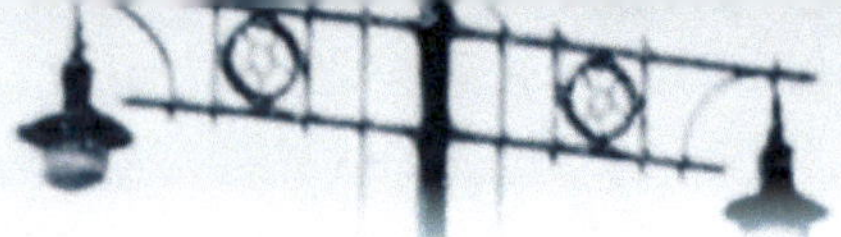

40. WESTWICK STREET

The junction between Saint Benedict's Street on the left and Westwick Street on the right has always been a difficult one. The large building at the bottom of the hill and the tower are part of Bullard's Anchor Brewery, one of the four big breweries of Norwich that were swallowed up by Watney Mann in the 1960s. The brewery, which is by the river, has been converted to apartments, but the chimney could not be saved.

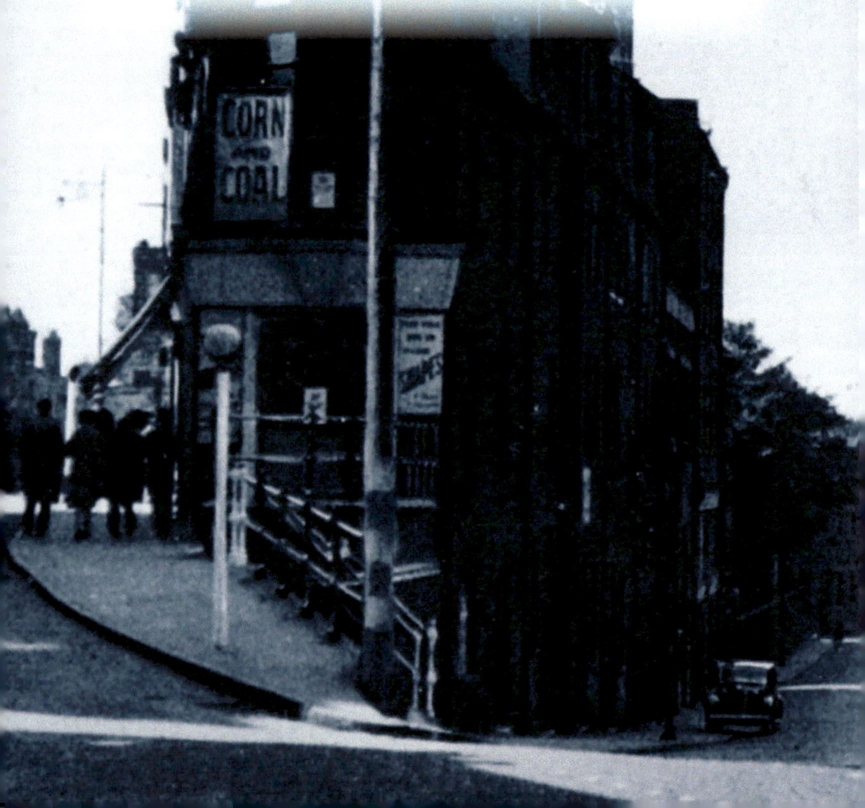

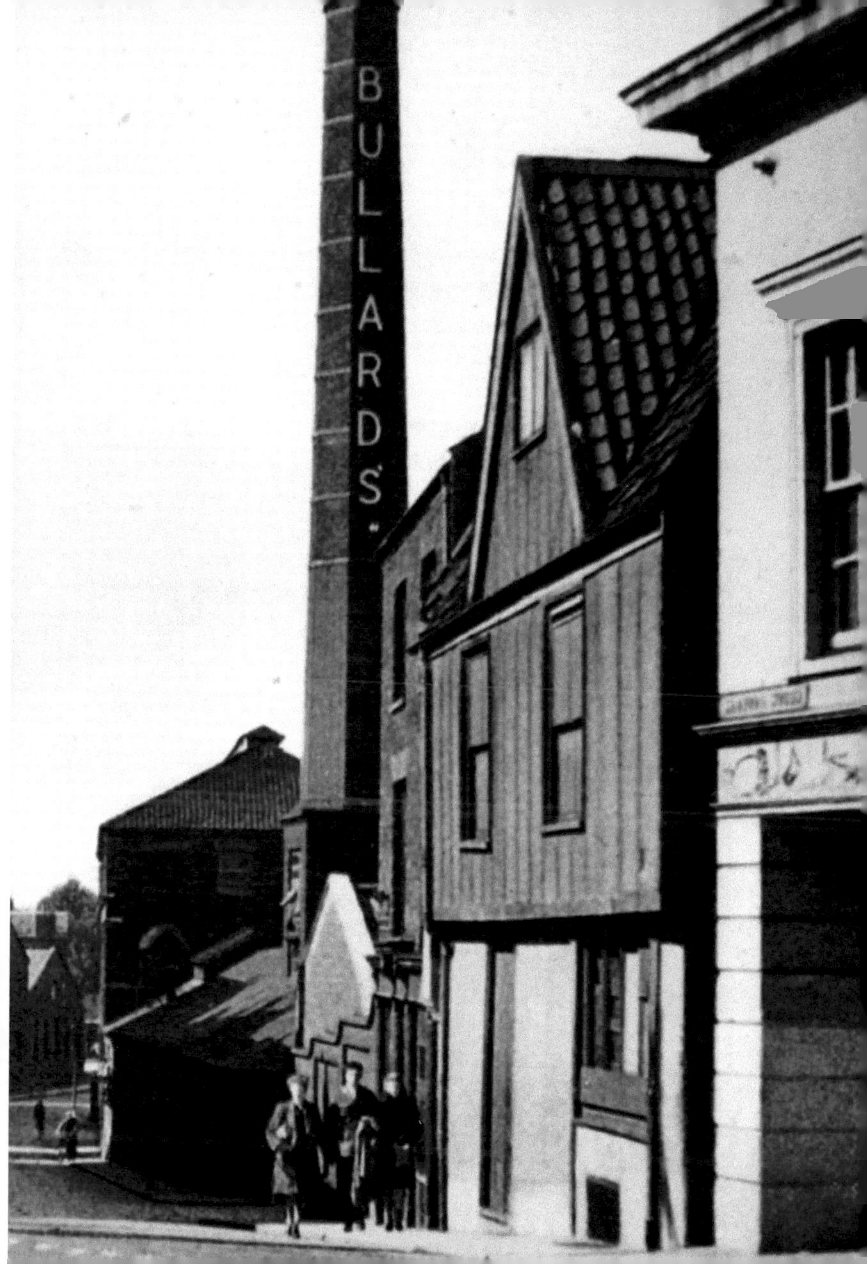

BULLARD'S.

41. COSLANY STREET

Norwich had a large number of shoe factories in the nineteenth and earlier twentieth centuries. Some of the names are world-famous, such as Bally and Start-rite. This building is the Sexton, Son & Everard factory in Coslany. The large factories have now closed. Some have been demolished like Howlett and White on Silver Road, but some have been 'recycled', such as this one, which is now split into several smaller businesses, including a snooker club.

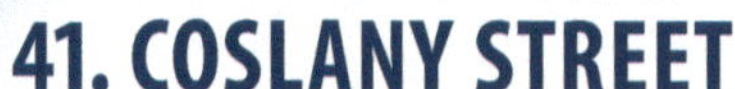

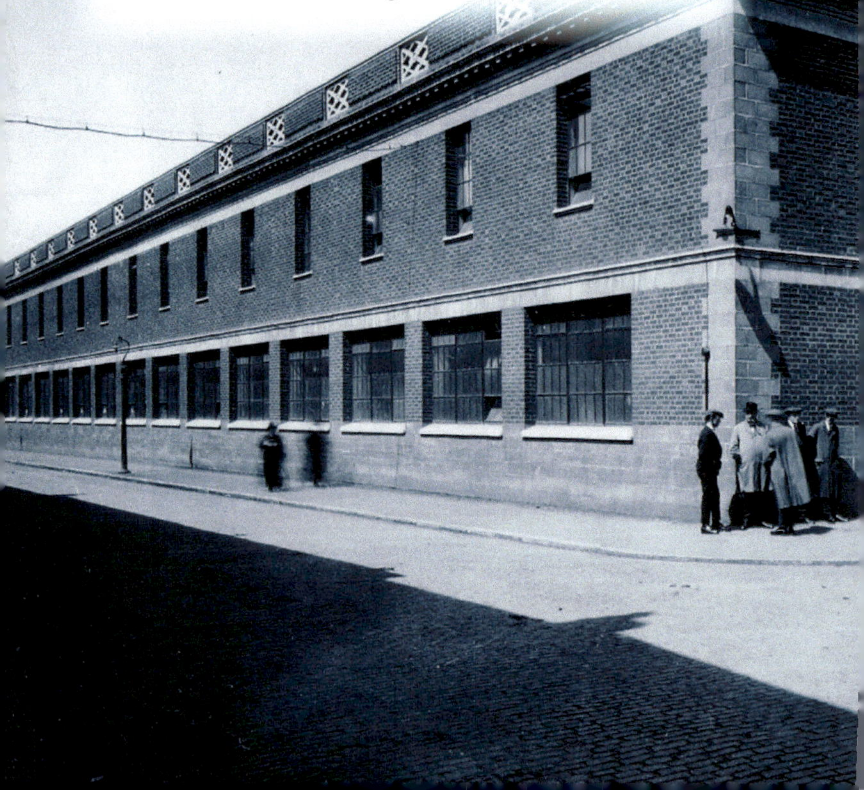

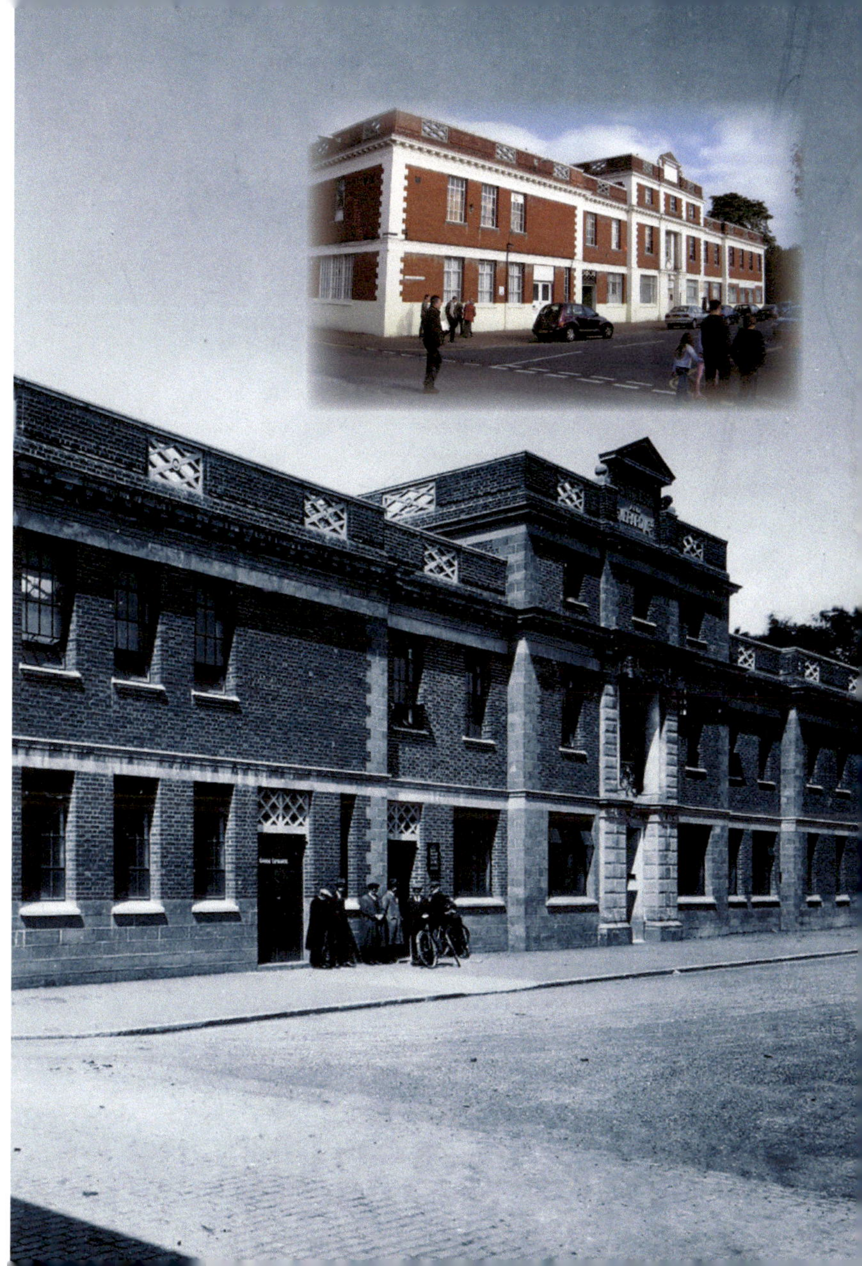

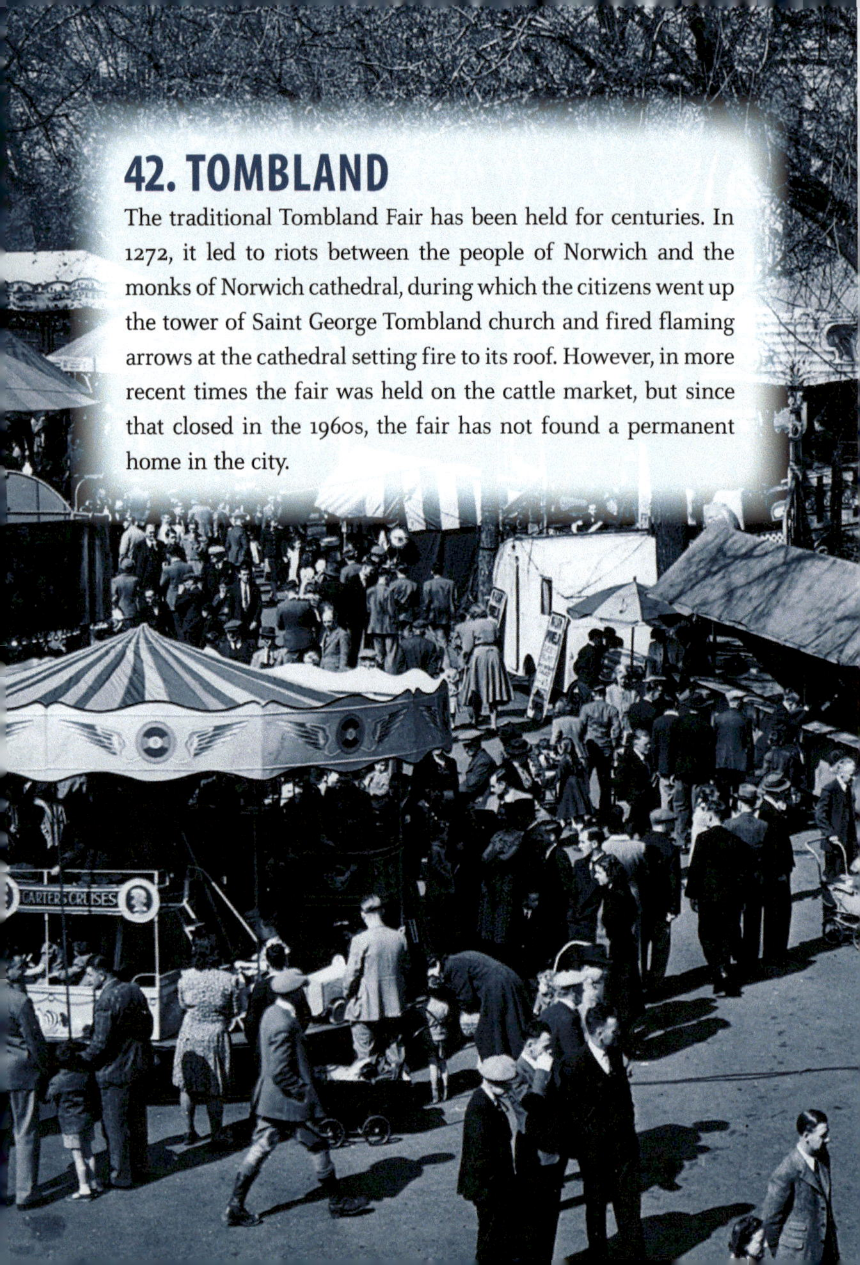

42. TOMBLAND

The traditional Tombland Fair has been held for centuries. In 1272, it led to riots between the people of Norwich and the monks of Norwich cathedral, during which the citizens went up the tower of Saint George Tombland church and fired flaming arrows at the cathedral setting fire to its roof. However, in more recent times the fair was held on the cattle market, but since that closed in the 1960s, the fair has not found a permanent home in the city.

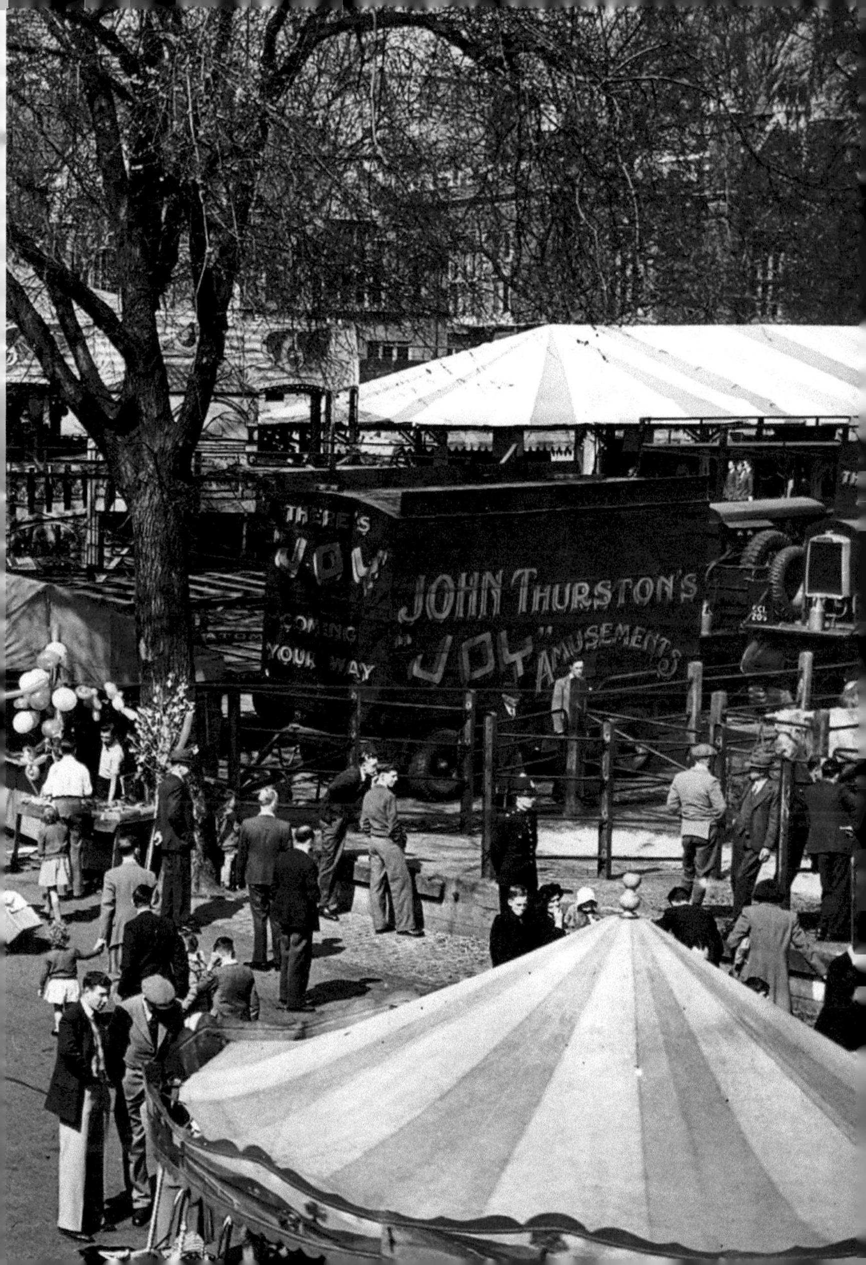

THERE'S
JOY
COMING
YOUR WAY
JOHN THURSTON'S
"JOY"
AMUSEMENTS

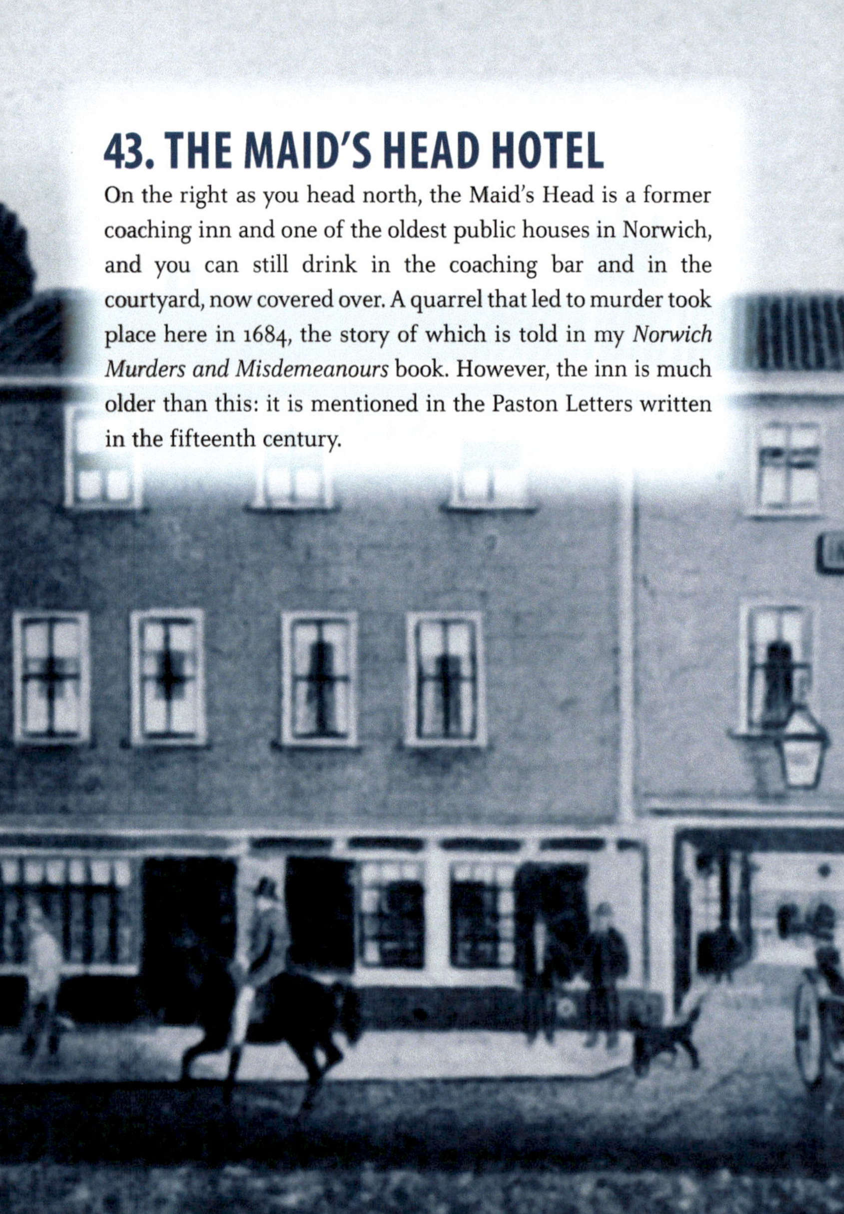

43. THE MAID'S HEAD HOTEL

On the right as you head north, the Maid's Head is a former coaching inn and one of the oldest public houses in Norwich, and you can still drink in the coaching bar and in the courtyard, now covered over. A quarrel that led to murder took place here in 1684, the story of which is told in my *Norwich Murders and Misdemeanours* book. However, the inn is much older than this: it is mentioned in the Paston Letters written in the fifteenth century.

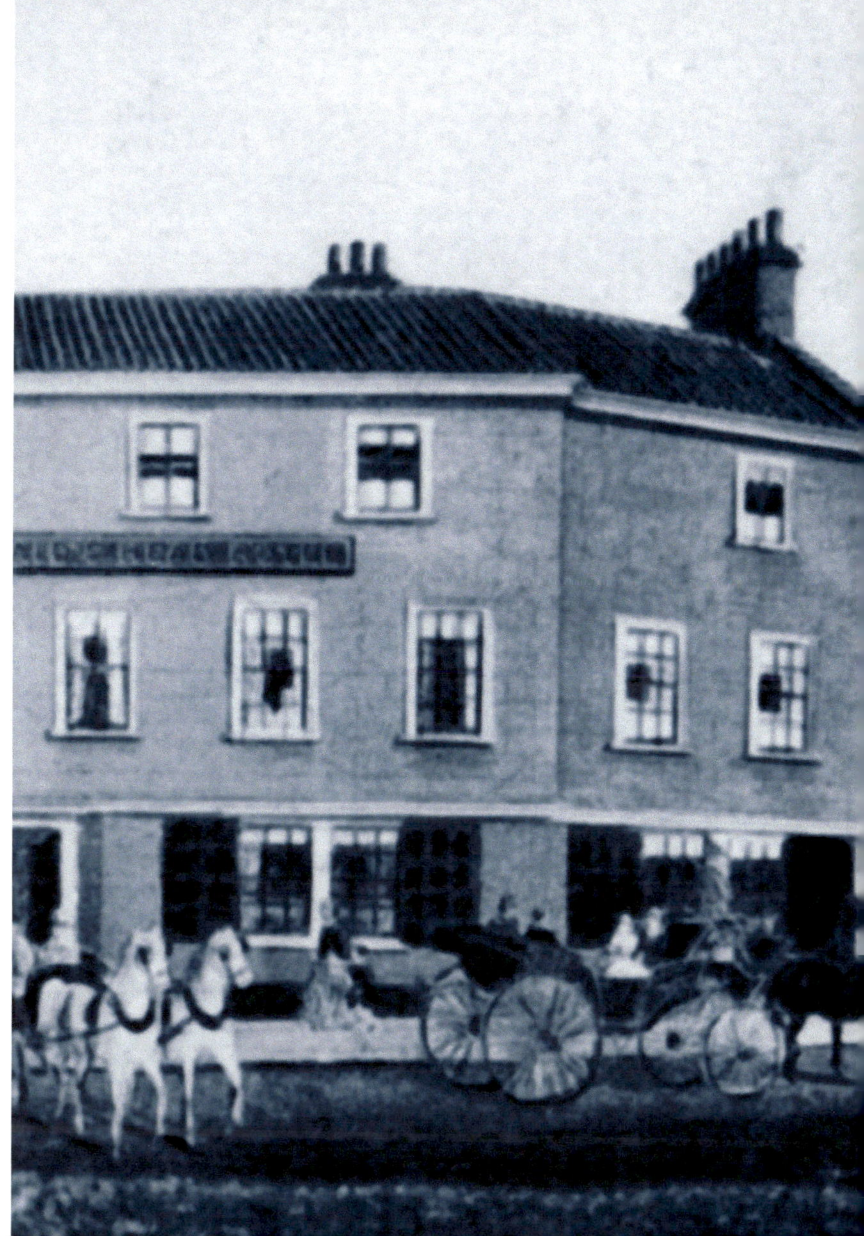

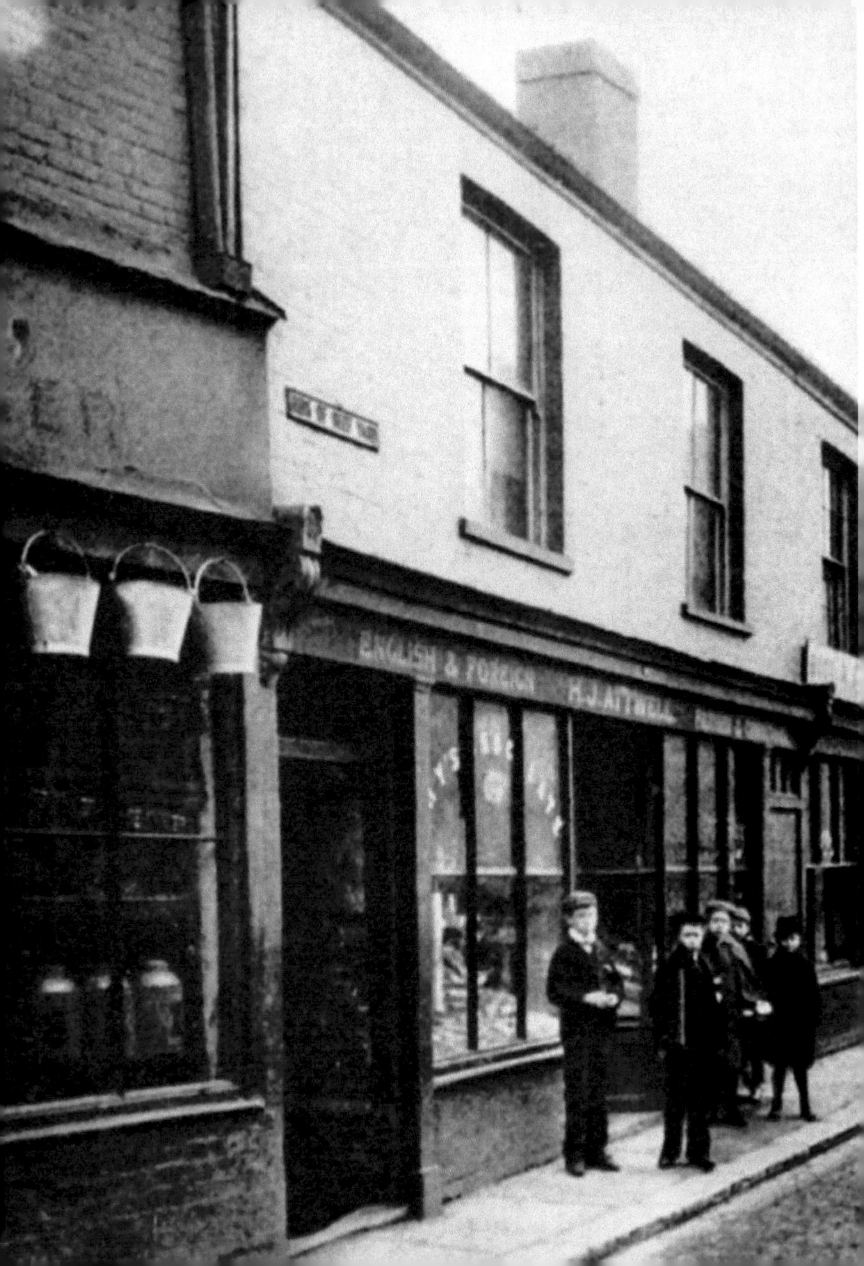

ENGLISH & FOREIGN
H.J. ATTWELL

44. FYE BRIDGE STREET

The river is crossed by Fye Bridge, one of the oldest crossing points in the city. Its name probably comes from the word *fyeing* meaning cleaning (the river). It needed it: in the great fires in Norwich in 1507, the flames spread across to the north part of the city on garbage that was filling up the river. The bridge in the historic photograph was replaced with a wider one in the 1930s.

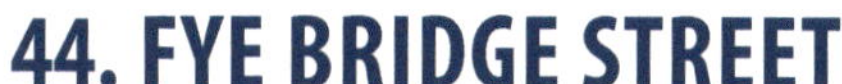

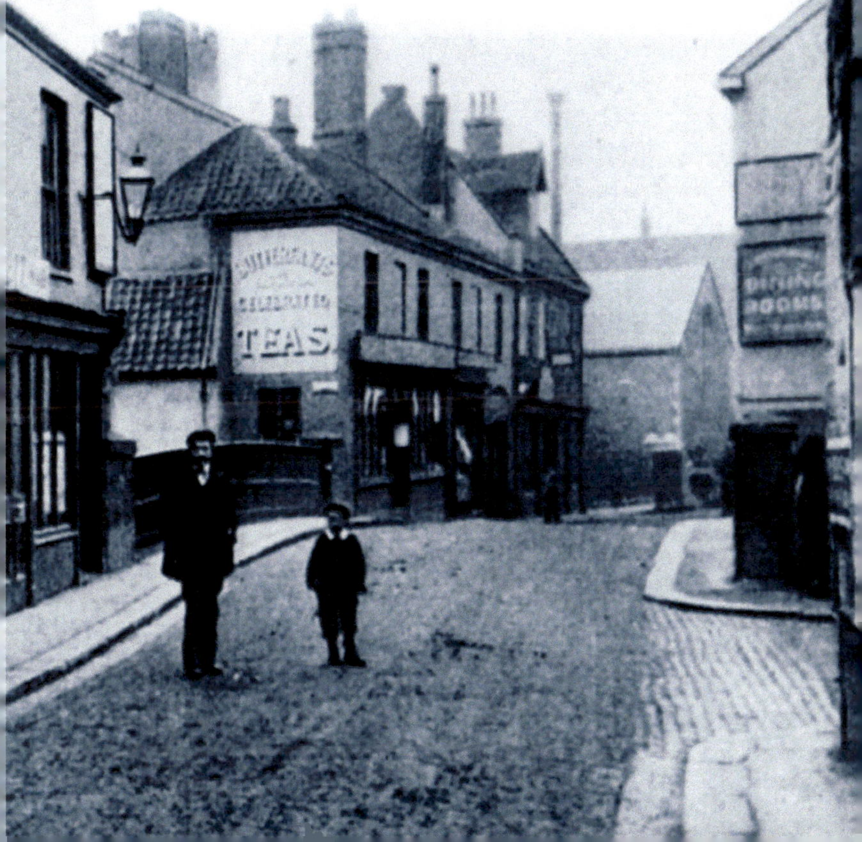

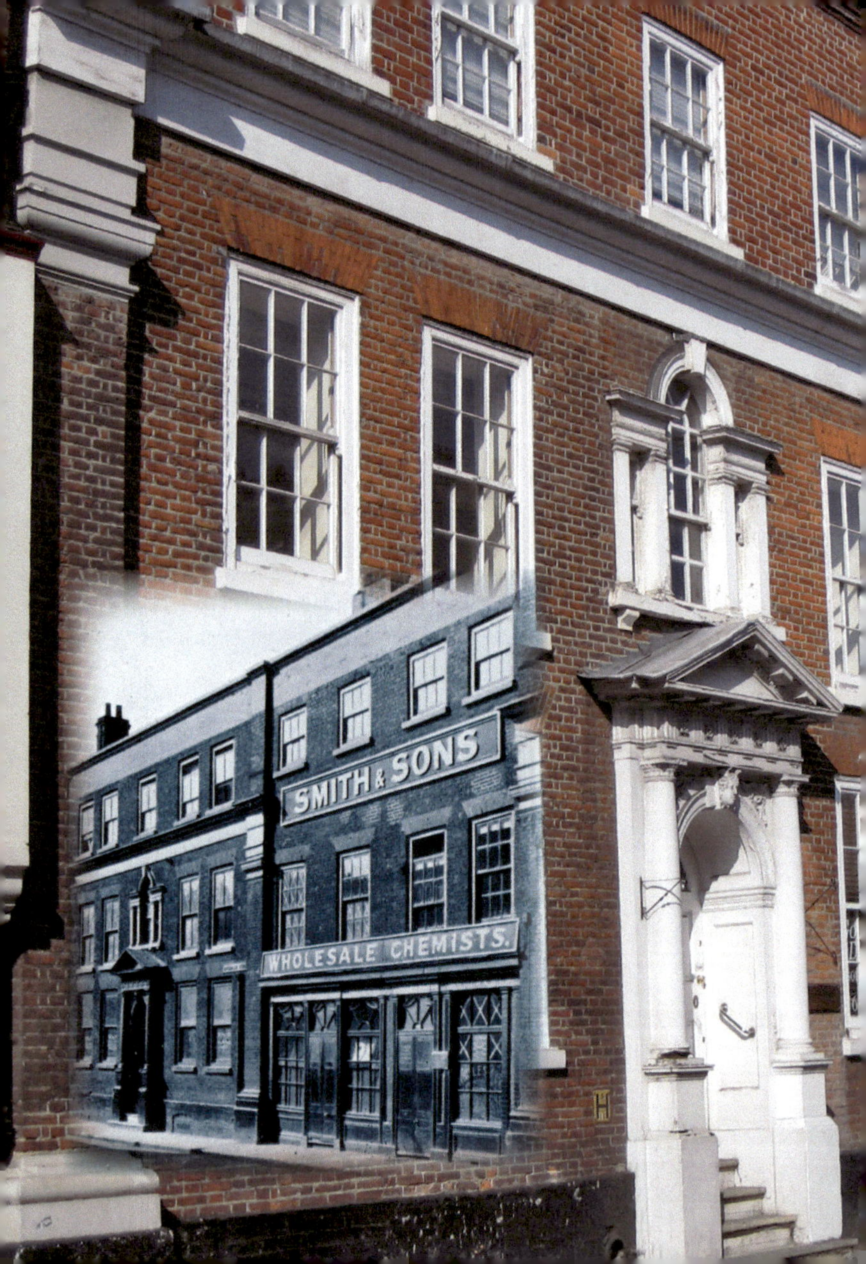

SMITH & SONS
WHOLESALE CHEMISTS.

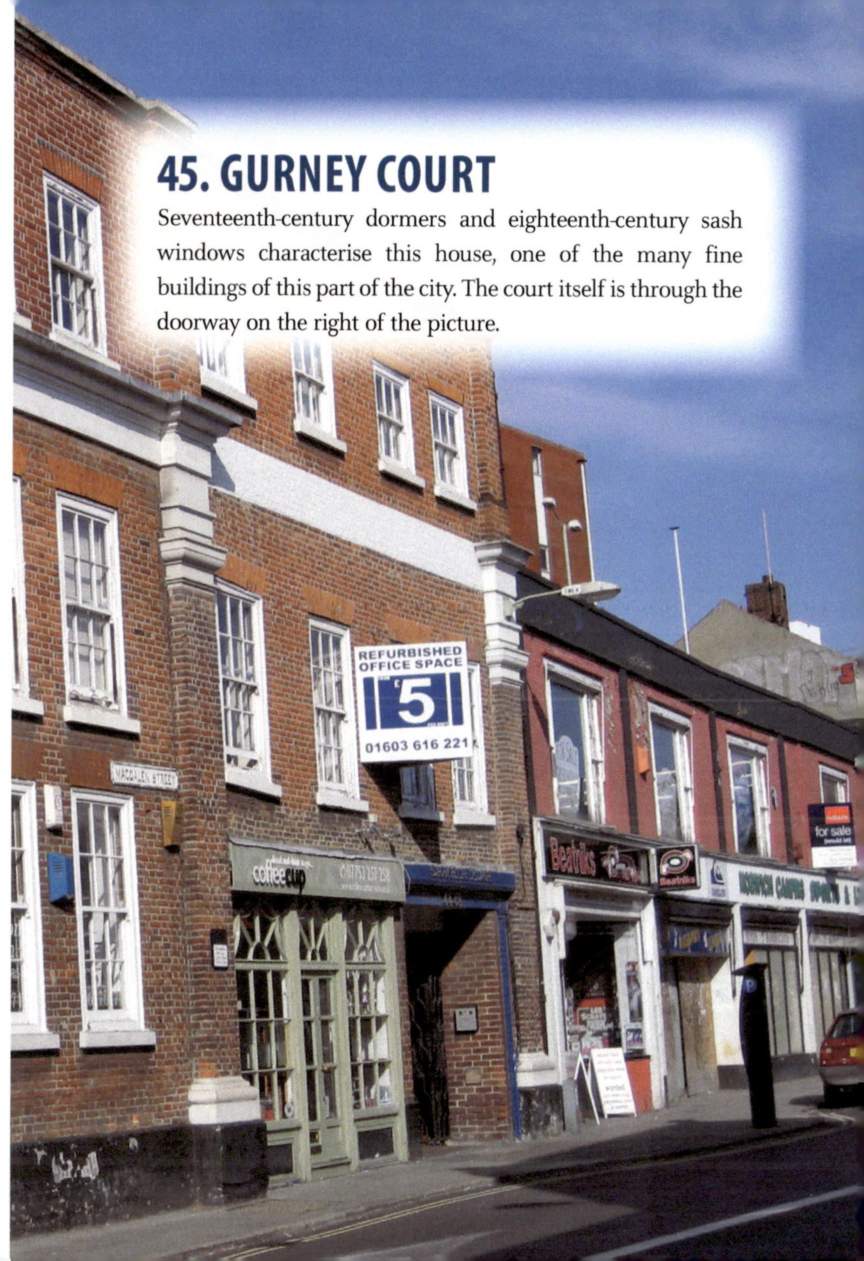

45. GURNEY COURT

Seventeenth-century dormers and eighteenth-century sash windows characterise this house, one of the many fine buildings of this part of the city. The court itself is through the doorway on the right of the picture.

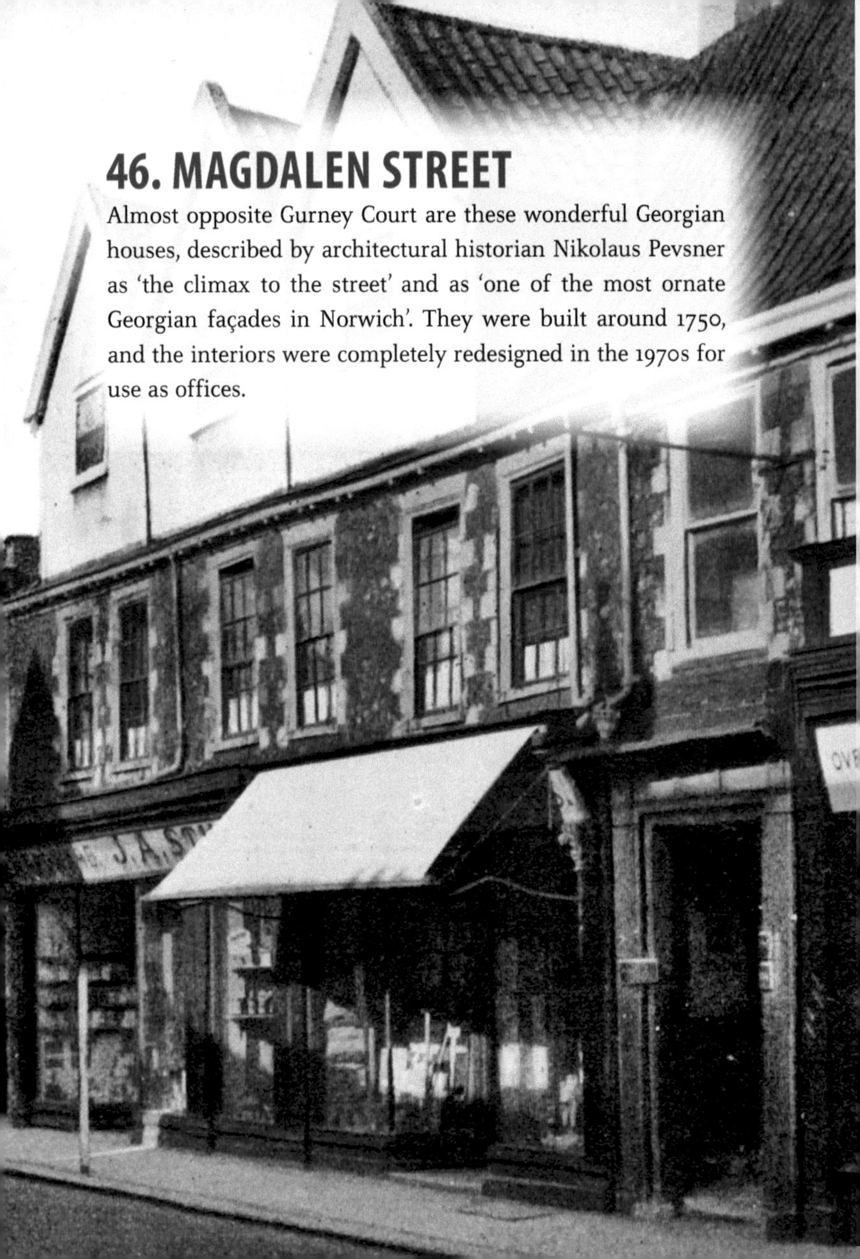

46. MAGDALEN STREET

Almost opposite Gurney Court are these wonderful Georgian houses, described by architectural historian Nikolaus Pevsner as 'the climax to the street' and as 'one of the most ornate Georgian façades in Norwich'. They were built around 1750, and the interiors were completely redesigned in the 1970s for use as offices.

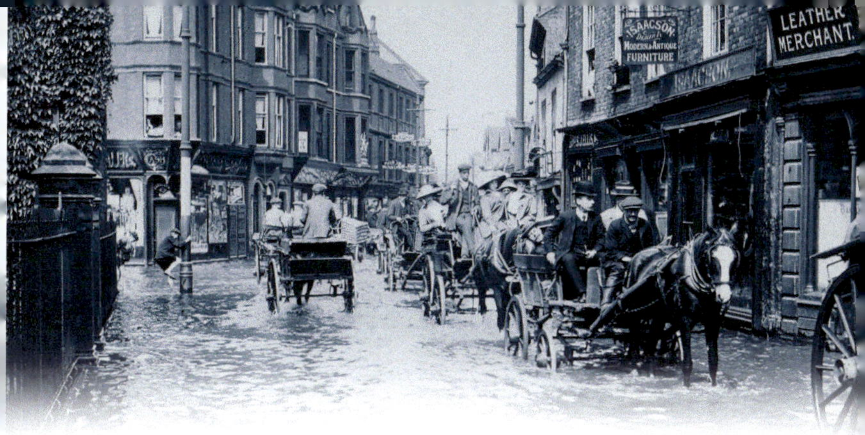

47. MAGDALEN STREET

The church on the left is that of Saint Clement. This was the heart of Viking Norwich in the late ninth century. The channel of the river in the city has been widened in the twentieth century and there has been no repeat of the disastrous flood of 1912 – so far!

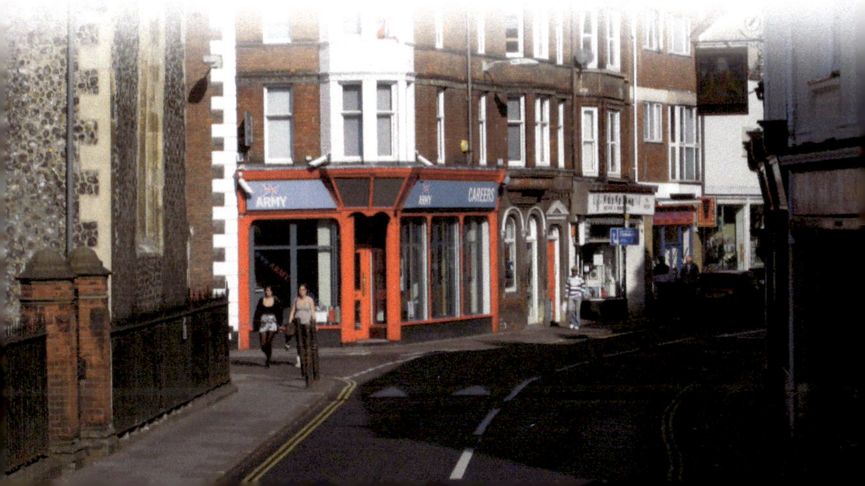

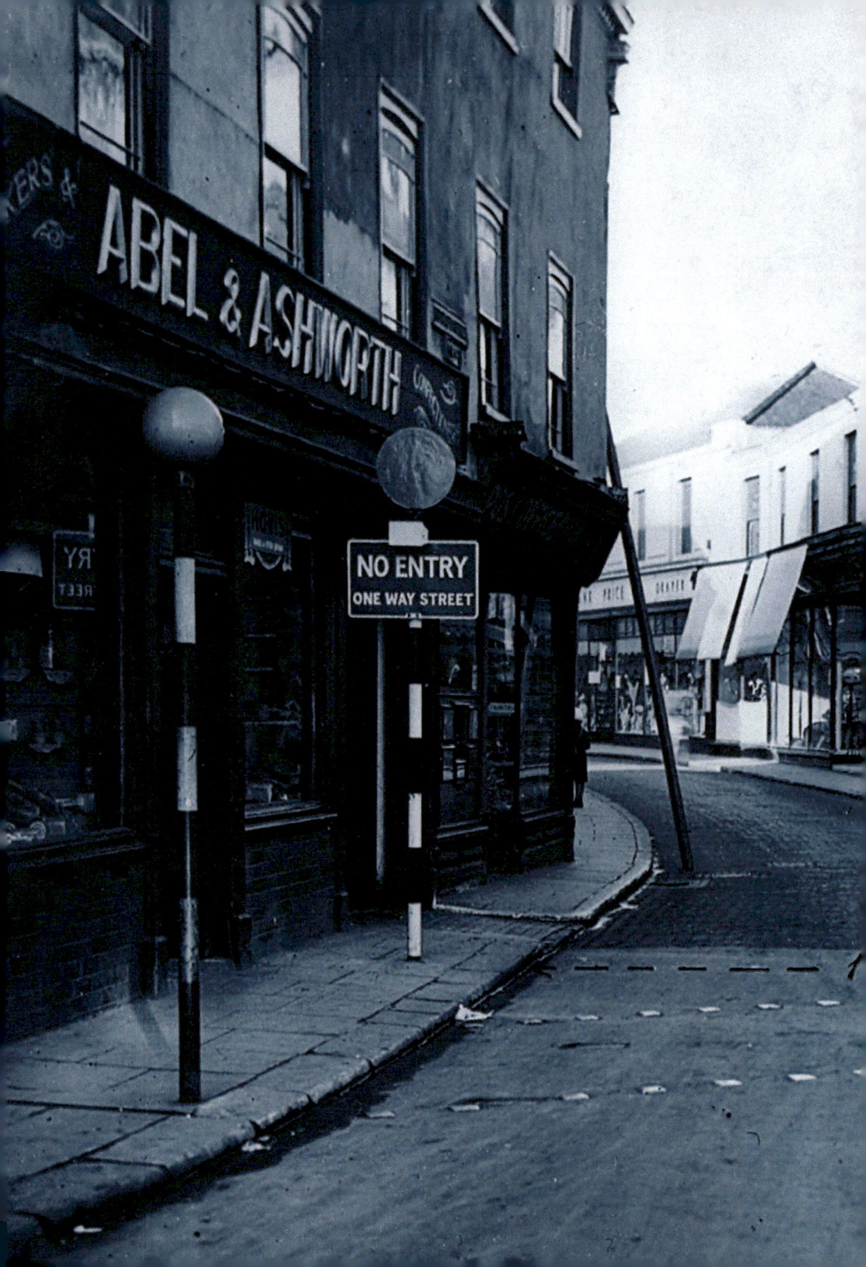

ABEL & ASHWORTH
NO ENTRY
ONE WAY STREET

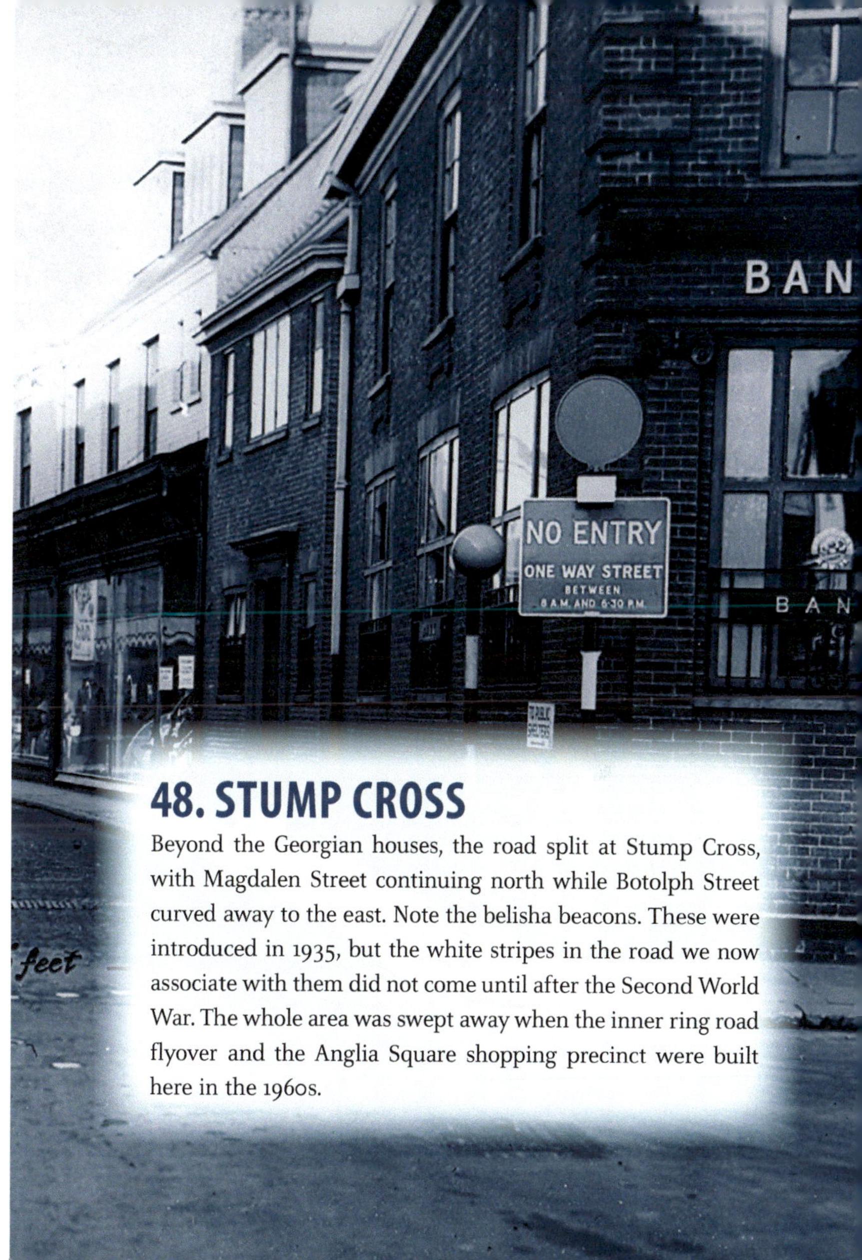

48. STUMP CROSS

Beyond the Georgian houses, the road split at Stump Cross, with Magdalen Street continuing north while Botolph Street curved away to the east. Note the belisha beacons. These were introduced in 1935, but the white stripes in the road we now associate with them did not come until after the Second World War. The whole area was swept away when the inner ring road flyover and the Anglia Square shopping precinct were built here in the 1960s.

49. NORWICH INSTITUTE FOR THE BLIND

The Norwich Institution for the Blind was founded over 200 years ago by Norwich ironmonger Thomas Tawell. It has continued to offer a wonderful service for the blind and the partially sighted, adapting to changing attitudes over the years. It is now called the Norfolk & Norwich Association for the Blind. In the nineteenth century, the main front was here on Magdalen Street, but this has been sold for new houses, and the present entrance is around the corner on Magpie Road.

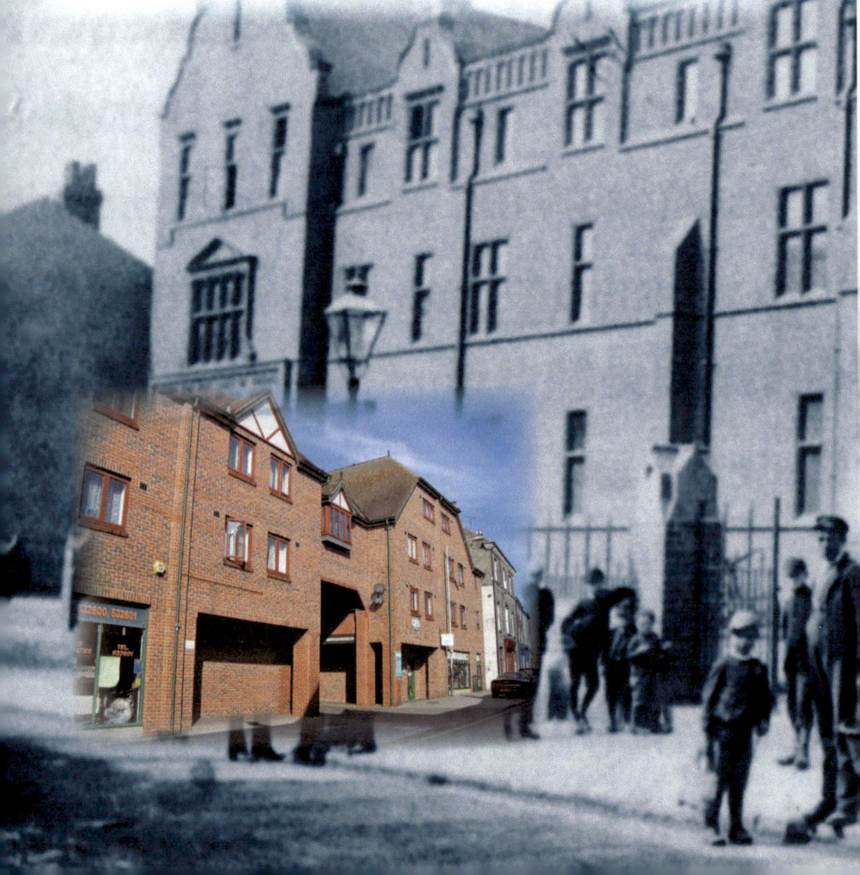

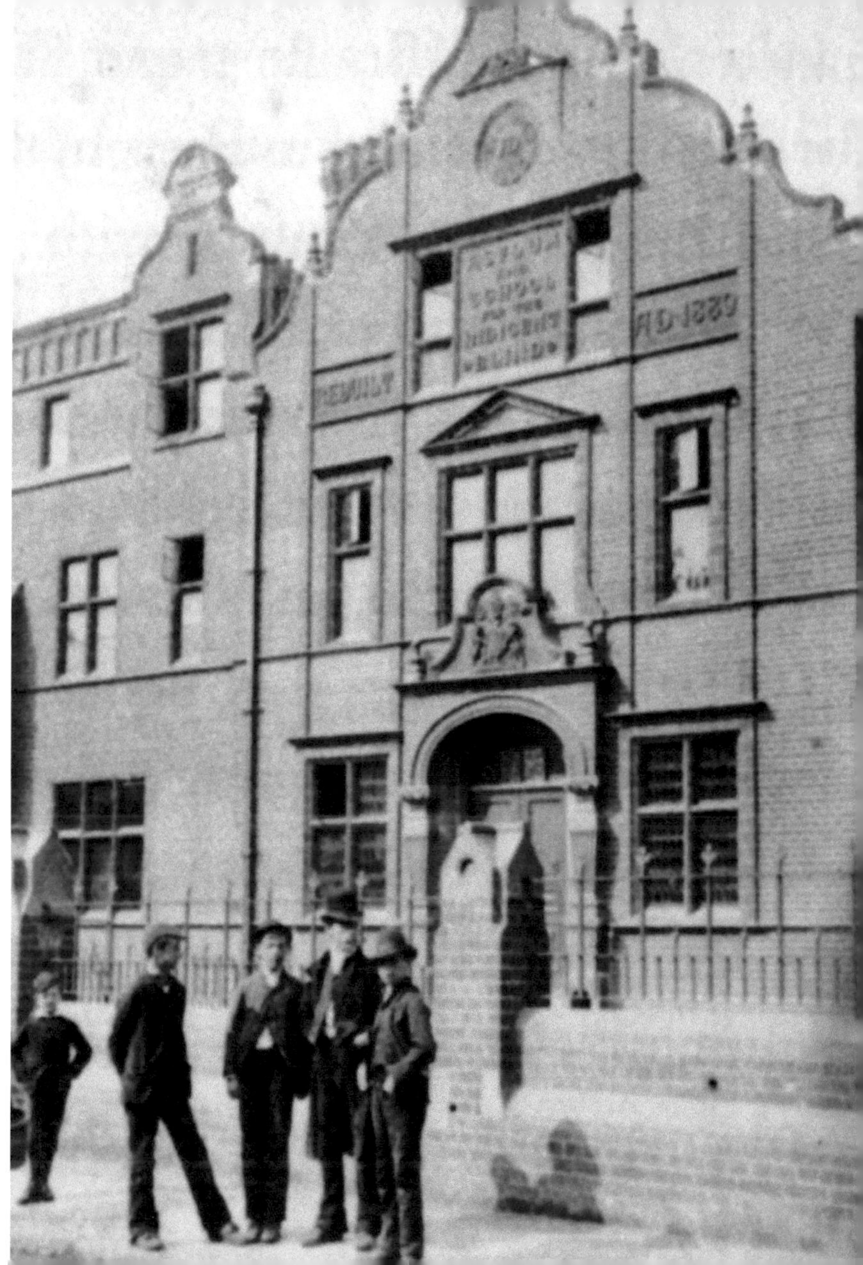

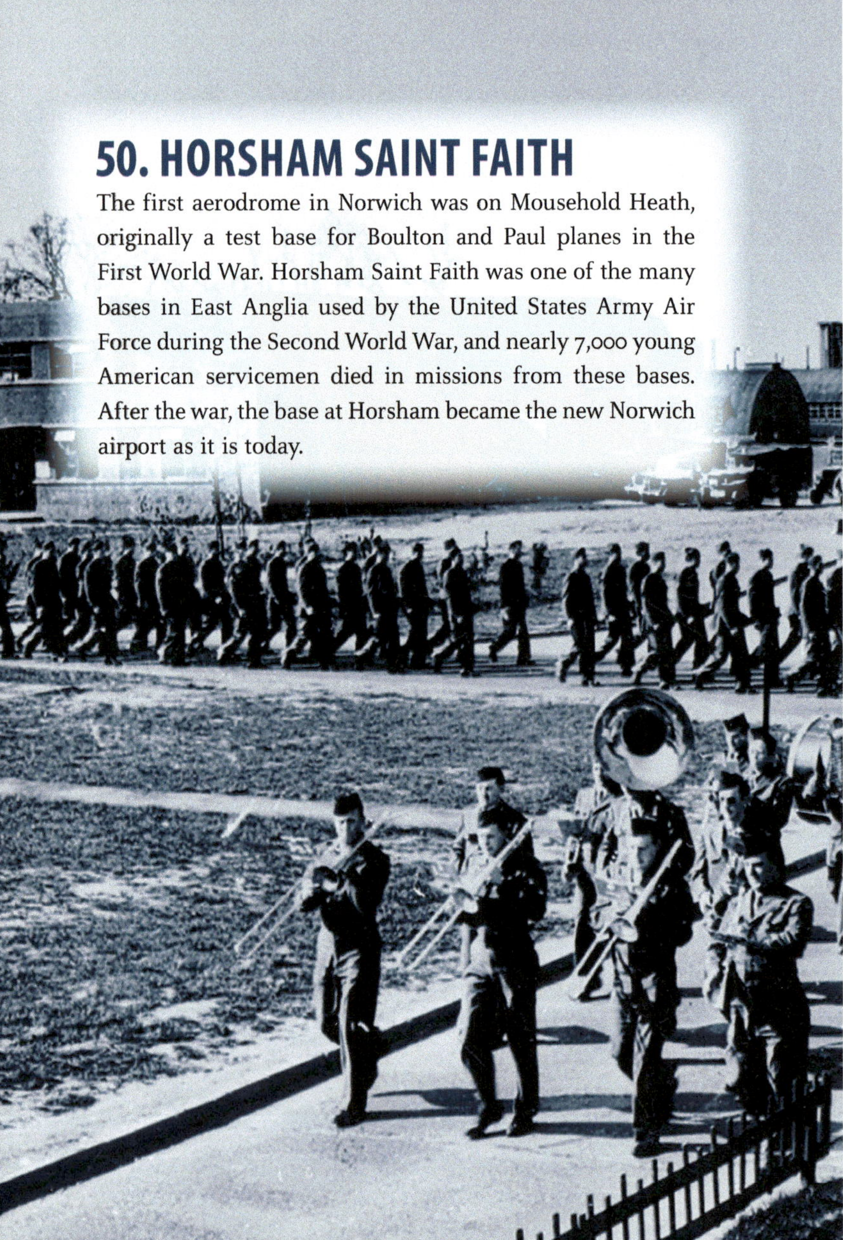

50. HORSHAM SAINT FAITH

The first aerodrome in Norwich was on Mousehold Heath, originally a test base for Boulton and Paul planes in the First World War. Horsham Saint Faith was one of the many bases in East Anglia used by the United States Army Air Force during the Second World War, and nearly 7,000 young American servicemen died in missions from these bases. After the war, the base at Horsham became the new Norwich airport as it is today.

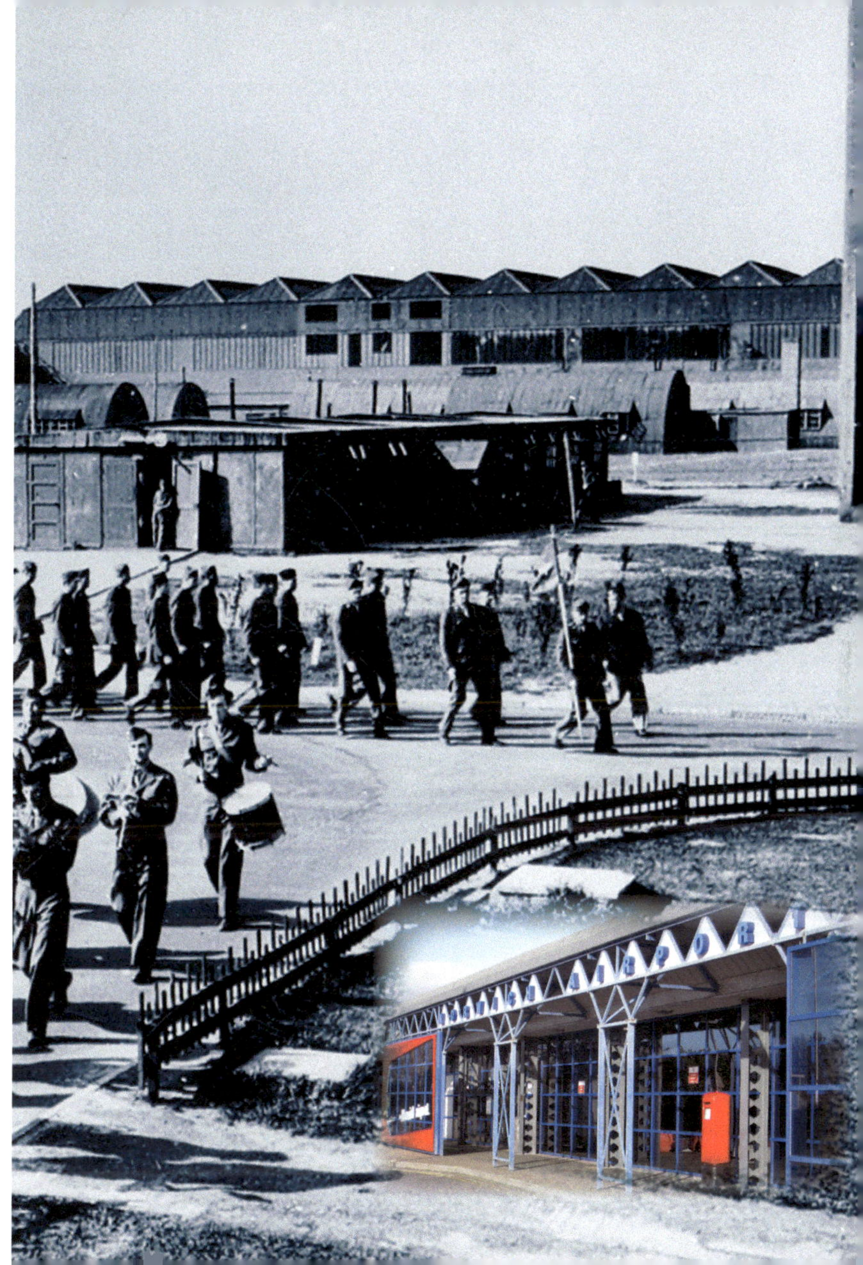
AIRPORT

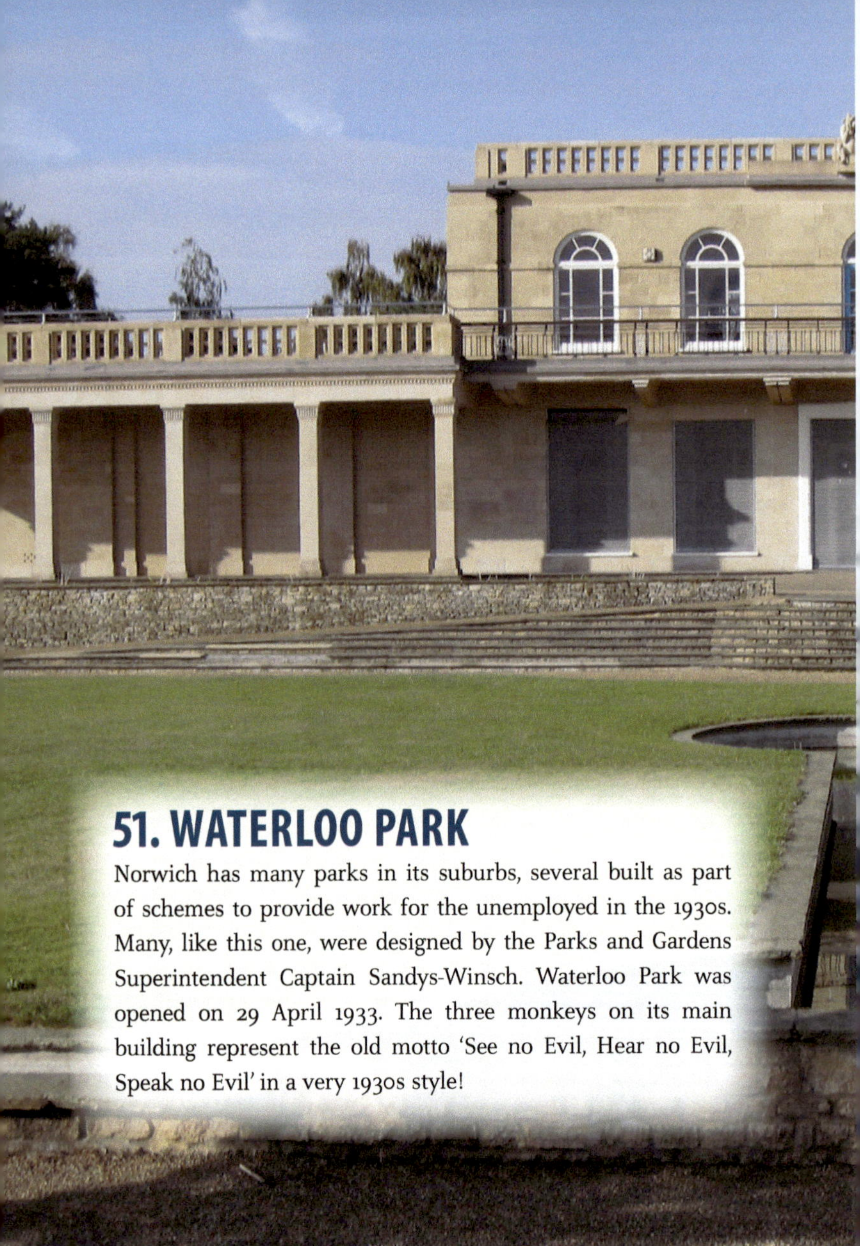

51. WATERLOO PARK

Norwich has many parks in its suburbs, several built as part of schemes to provide work for the unemployed in the 1930s. Many, like this one, were designed by the Parks and Gardens Superintendent Captain Sandys-Winsch. Waterloo Park was opened on 29 April 1933. The three monkeys on its main building represent the old motto 'See no Evil, Hear no Evil, Speak no Evil' in a very 1930s style!

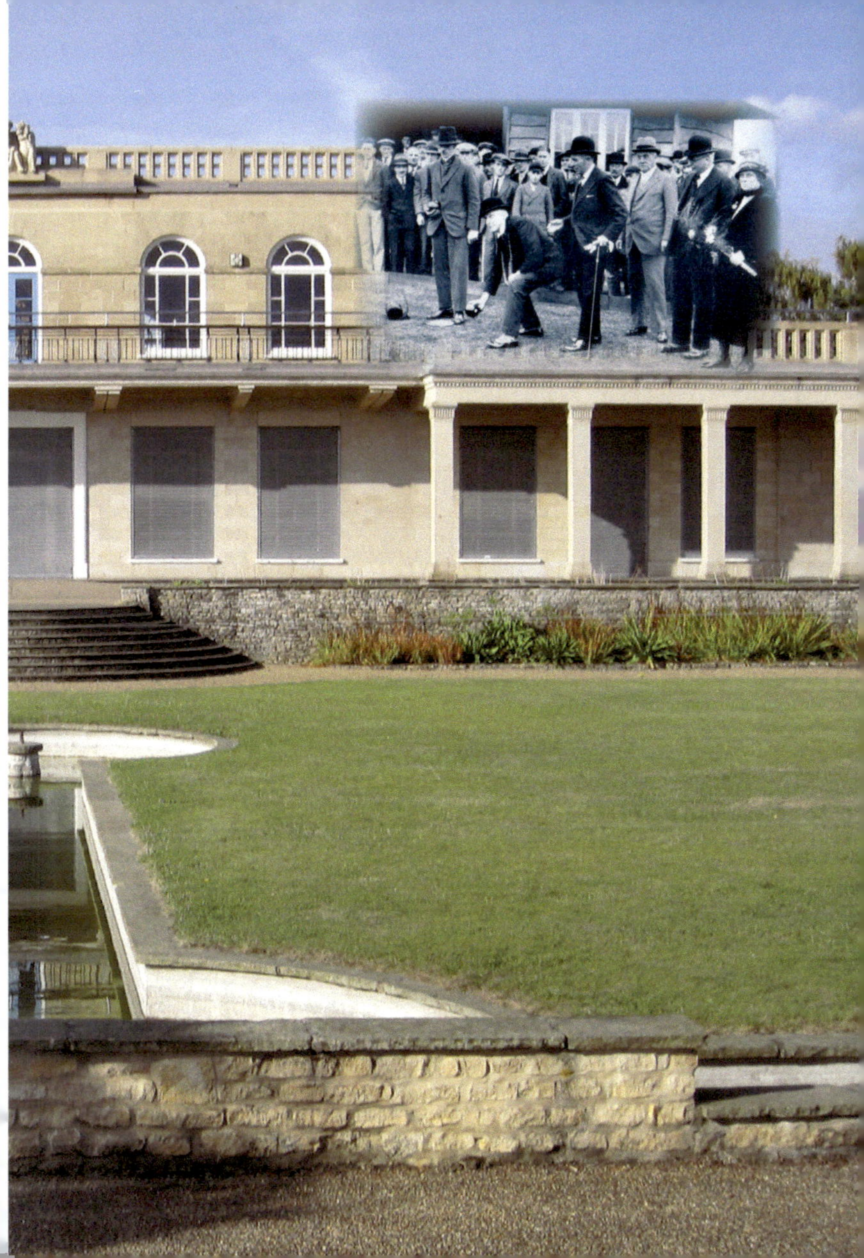

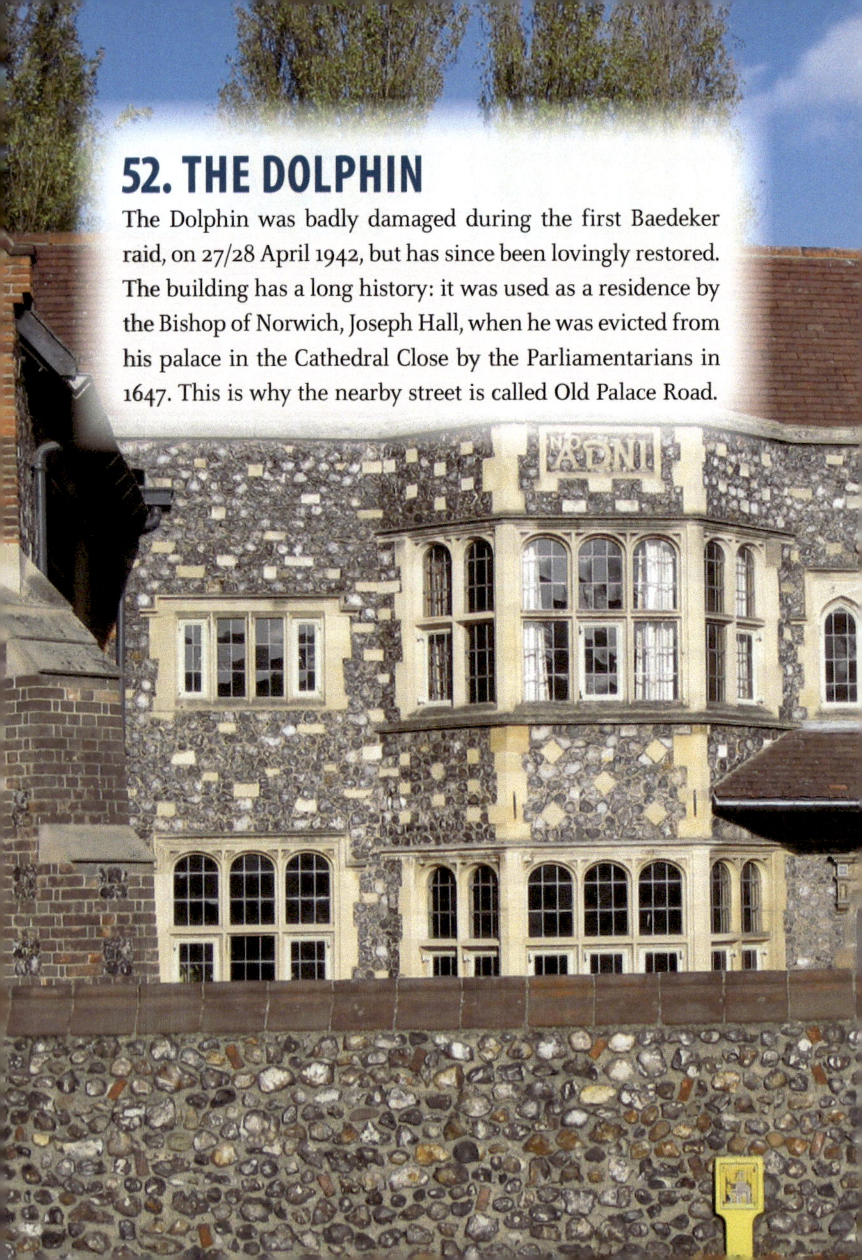

52. THE DOLPHIN

The Dolphin was badly damaged during the first Baedeker raid, on 27/28 April 1942, but has since been lovingly restored. The building has a long history: it was used as a residence by the Bishop of Norwich, Joseph Hall, when he was evicted from his palace in the Cathedral Close by the Parliamentarians in 1647. This is why the nearby street is called Old Palace Road.

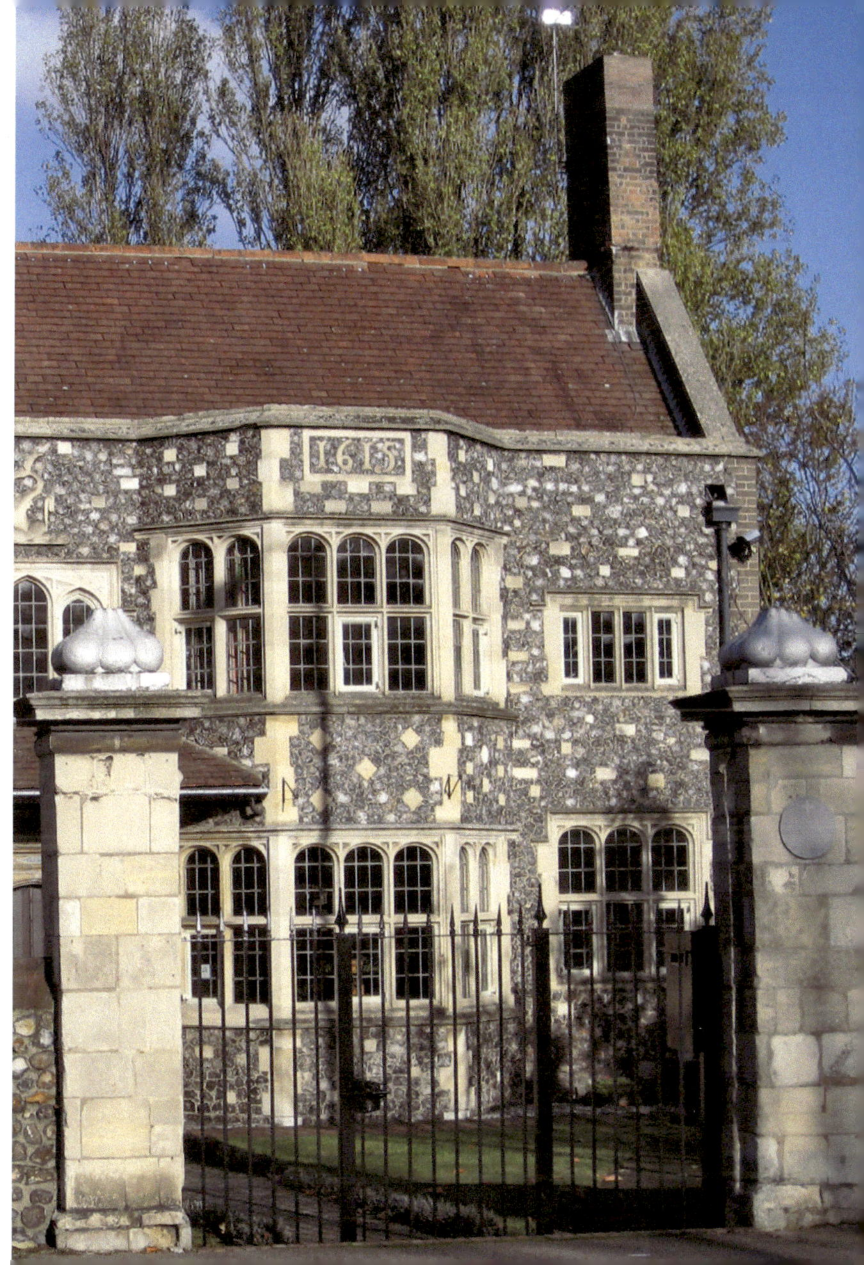

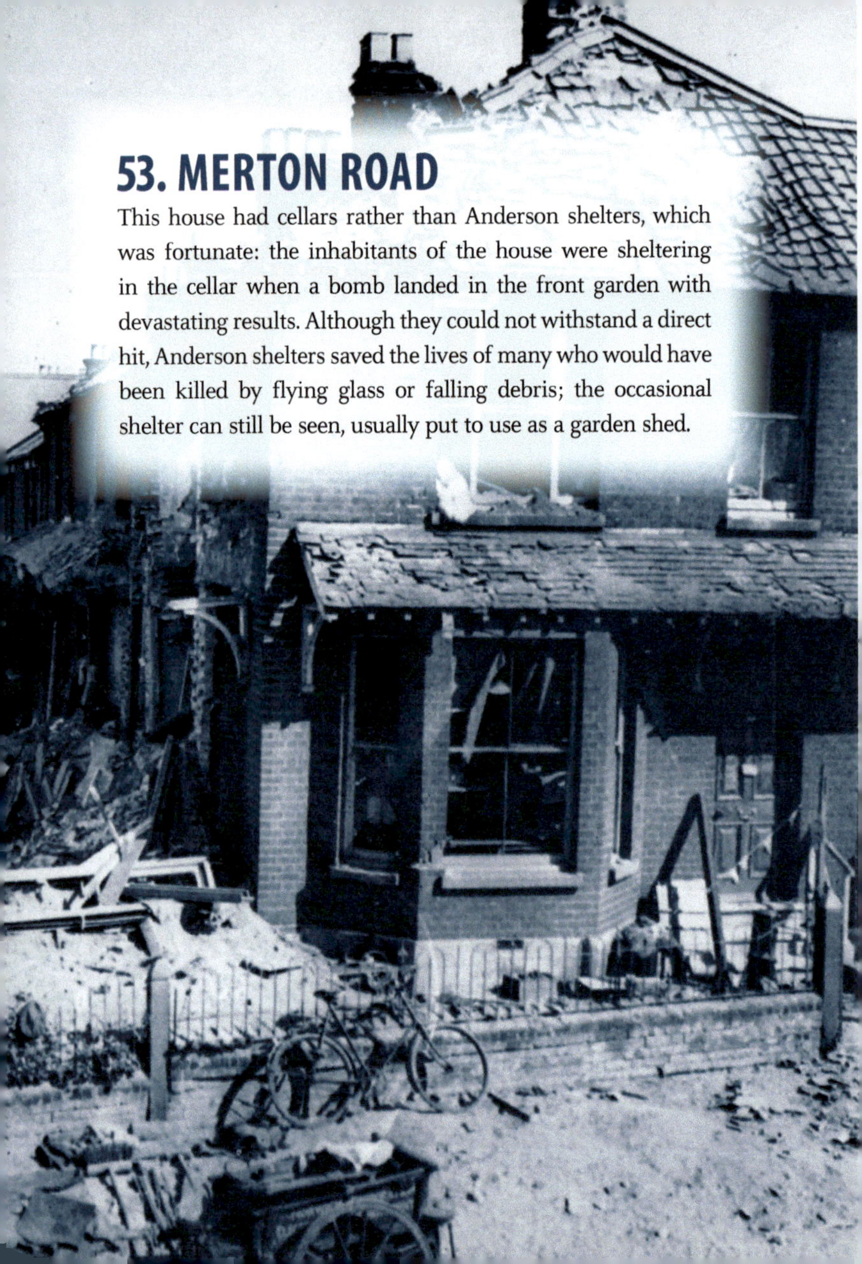

53. MERTON ROAD

This house had cellars rather than Anderson shelters, which was fortunate: the inhabitants of the house were sheltering in the cellar when a bomb landed in the front garden with devastating results. Although they could not withstand a direct hit, Anderson shelters saved the lives of many who would have been killed by flying glass or falling debris; the occasional shelter can still be seen, usually put to use as a garden shed.

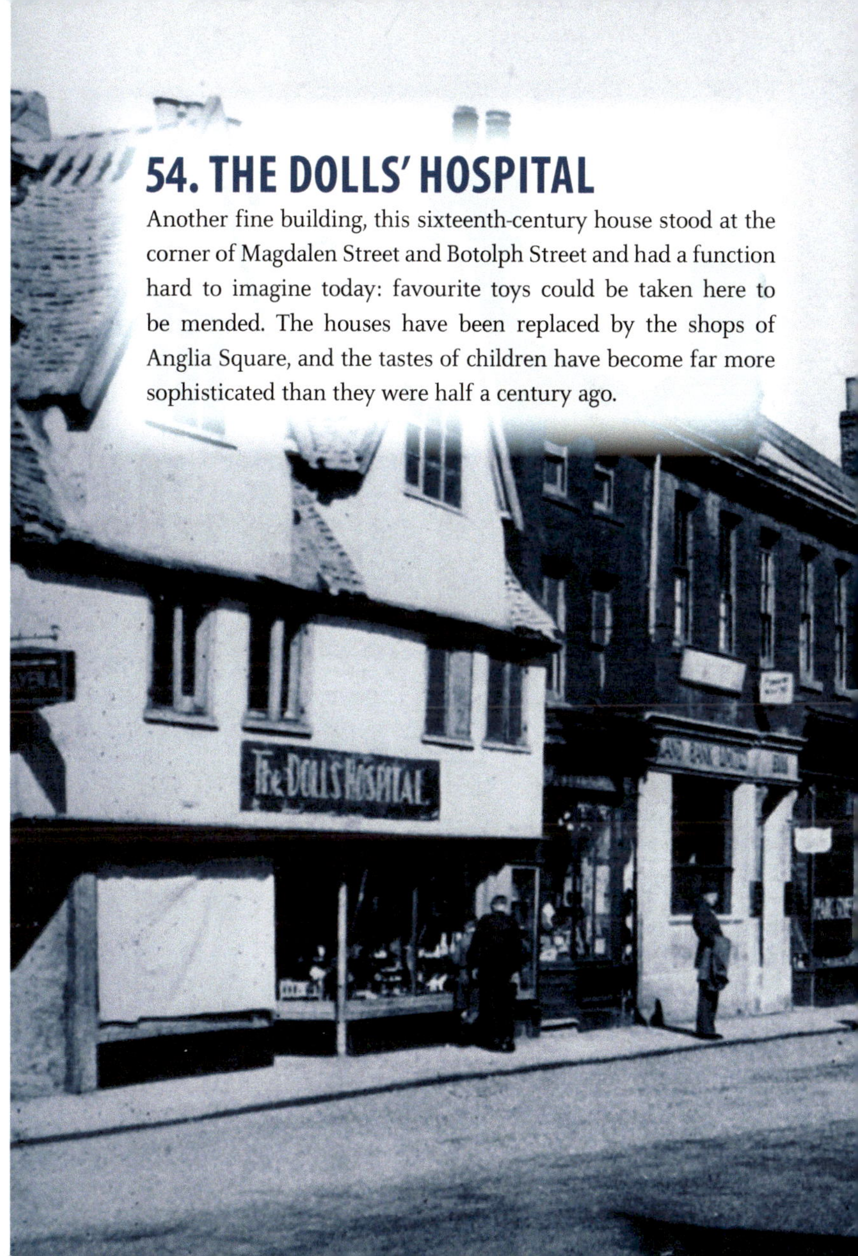

54. THE DOLLS' HOSPITAL

Another fine building, this sixteenth-century house stood at the corner of Magdalen Street and Botolph Street and had a function hard to imagine today: favourite toys could be taken here to be mended. The houses have been replaced by the shops of Anglia Square, and the tastes of children have become far more sophisticated than they were half a century ago.

ACKNOWLEDGEMENTS

Many of the historic photographs are from sources at the Norfolk Record Office; I am grateful to Dr John Alban, County Archivist, for permission to use these images.

Several images are from the photograph collection of the United States Army Air Force held at the Record Office (reference MC 371/908). I am grateful to the American Memorial Library in Norwich for permission to use these photographs.

Norfolk Record Office colleagues also helped. Thank you to Edwin King for two historic photographs, to Victoria Horth for two modern images, and to Tom Townsend for the modern image of the Guildhall, under scaffolding when this book was in preparation.